MATH TO THE

MUSIC

MATH TO THE MUSIC

A NUMBEROCK WORKBOOK

GRADE 4

Benjamin Hehn

Rebecca McDonagh

JB JOSSEY-BASS™

A Wiley Brand

Library of Congress Cataloging-in-Publication Data is Available:
ISBN 978-1-394-36435-0 (Paperback)
ISBN 978-1-394-36436-7 (ePDF)
ISBN 978-1-394-36437-4 (ePub)

Cover Design: Wiley
Cover character art by Numberock
Printed and bound by CPI Group (UK) Ltd, Croydon, CR0 4YY

C9781394364350_220426

For Lexi and Ellis, whose love remind me daily why I do this work. For my students of the past, present, and future, and for every teacher bold enough to try something unconventional and bring their art into their teaching. May this book be a reminder that your creativity matters.
–Benjamin

This book is dedicated to Charlotte and Finn; your laughter, questions, and love taught me more about teaching than any textbook ever could. To R.S. for your love and encouragement. Your rose-colored glasses never come off and I am eternally grateful for you. To D.C. who is the catalyst for this whole new chapter in my life. You knew I could do it before I ever even dreamed it. And to Mom, Dad and Boo who never think my ideas are too crazy and are always along for the ride.
–Rebecca

Contents

Acknowledgments

To Dr. Anne Foley, thank you for seeing the power of creativity in the classroom and for allowing me to bring a piano, guitar, and drum set into school, which ended up being a decision that changed the course of my life. To Carmina Scuccimara, my mentor teacher, who modeled rigor, high expectations, and the joy of watching students grow. To my mother, Ginette Hehn, and my wife, Lexi, for being my editors, advisors, and most trusted sounding boards. To my brother, Dave, whose encouragement and practical help made it possible to turn my dream and passion for combining math and music into a career. To Robert A. Banning, for helping edit our manuscript and for his many valuable contributions and suggestions. To my colleague, Rebecca McDonagh: collaborating with you reminded me that the best teaching and the best art nearly always comes from collaboration.

–Benjamin

This book wouldn't exist without the incredible students who've danced, clapped, and sung their way through math lessons with me over the years – you are the true rock stars of this journey. To Ben, thank you for turning math into music and inspiring my students and me. I'm endlessly grateful to my fellow educators for cheering me on and believing in the power of creative teaching. Thank you to all the educators past and present who contributed their funny and heartwarming stories to this book and to my dear friend Vera who labored over each anchor chart with me. To my family and friends who celebrated every little win–your love and laughter kept me going. And finally, to every teacher who dares to make math magical: this book is for you.

–Rebecca

About the Authors

Benjamin Hehn is a former fifth-grade teacher turned songwriter, producer, and founder of Numberock, a company dedicated to making math memorable, applicable, and inspirational through music. His videos and songs have been used in classrooms across the globe, from Singapore's national curriculum to being featured by Discovery Education, Edutopia, Common Sense Media, and The Wall Street Journal. Hehn is also composing the theme song for the St. Jude Math-A-Thon, integrating his pursuit and love of combining music with math to benefit children in all walks of life. He lives with his wife, Lexi, and their son, Ellis, in Central Massachusetts, where God, family, a love of math and music, and curiosity guide him in his labor of love, Numberock.

Rebecca McDonagh has been inspiring young mathematicians for nearly two decades as a dedicated elementary math teacher. Named Teacher of the Year for her innovative and engaging approach to instruction, Rebecca brings numbers to life through rhythm and melody, helping students connect with math in a fun, memorable way. Her collaboration with Numberock on *Math to the Music* reflects her belief that learning should be joyful, creative, and accessible to all. Out of the classroom, Rebecca loves adventuring in her home state of Florida with her son, daughter and their sweet rescue dog, Foxy.

Introduction

A couple of years ago, Ben was driving home from the supermarket when he received a phone call from an unknown number. "Hi, this is Becca McDonagh!" came the cheerful voice on the other end. "I've been sharing your videos on my Instagram account and just wanted to tell you how awesome your songs are and how much my students love them." That quick 10-minute chat was filled with laughter and shared stories about teaching; and it ended with a notion that maybe someday we'd find a way to work together.

More than a year went by before the phone rang again. This time, Becca called with some serious enthusiasm and said, "Hey, I have a book idea . . . but I only want to do it if you'll do it with me!" At that point, Ben had a lot going on. He was in the midst of moving from Texas to Massachusetts, writing a theme song for the St. Jude Math-A-Thon, and was in the planning stage of rebuilding Numberock's website for the first time in over a decade, but there was no way he could turn down the project after listening to Becca's enthusiasm and conviction. Within days, we were brainstorming ideas, swapping notes, and dreaming about how we could bring math and music together in a book series.

What started as two teachers connecting over a shared love of teaching and creativity soon became *Math to the Music*, a book written by teachers, for teachers. From 15-minute planning calls that turned into multiple-hour phone discussions and lots of lengthy voice and text messages, to meetings with Jossey-Bass and Wiley, we moved into high gear fast and finalized our outline, mapped out our shared responsibilities, and finally finished our draft of Chapter 1 about a month later. From that point on, we were off to the races.

Ben's musical math curriculum found a perfect home in Becca's classroom, where anyone who tunes in to her Instagram channel can see that the art of teaching and learning can be full of laughter, rhythm, and motion. Together, we set out to capture that magic – her mix of wit, movement, and rigorous instruction that makes math come alive in her classroom. Our hope is that this book provides teachers with the practical tools and creative inspiration that allow students to experience math in a new way; not as something to memorize, but as something to feel, sing, dance to, and remember.

We hope you'll discover that when students learn "Math to the Music," something nearly magical happens. And that's when the learning sticks.

MATH TO THE

MUSIC

NUMBER AND OPERATIONS IN BASE TEN

Place Value and Rounding

Notes from the Classroom

As a math teacher, I always try to engage students and help them connect math to real-world experiences.

During our fractions unit a few years ago, I brought in a few pizzas and told the kids we'd be doing an activity before eating. I cut each pizza into different-sized slices and passed them out on paper plates, each plate labeled with the fraction of the whole that the slice on it represented. I then asked my students to move around the room and find someone with a bigger or smaller slice than they had so they could compare fractions and the sizes of the slices.

As they rotated and discussed, I circulated and asked guiding questions. Toward the end, I came to a pair of boys arguing about whose piece was bigger. They were comparing slices meant to represent 1/4 and 1/6, but their pieces were almost exactly the same size. I thought maybe I had cut one of the pizzas incorrectly or labeled the plate wrong until I noticed tiny teeth marks all up and down one slice.

Apparently someone had been too hungry to wait and tried to nibble just enough off one side to keep me from noticing (and tide themselves over until they were allowed to eat)! The next year, I learned my lesson and told the kids the pizzas were made with anchovies until I was ready for them to actually chow down!

–Miss K
Sunnyville, OH

Section 1: Place Value of Whole Numbers

In this section, we'll dive into digits in multidigit whole numbers to understand how digits relate to one another, focusing on the idea that a digit in one place is worth ten times the value of the same digit in the place to its right. We'll also practice reading and writing numbers up to one million in standard form, expanded form, and word form. Get ready to take an adventure with Rob to his favorite blueberry patch, and then join him on a journey to the Incan ruins of Machu Picchu in Numberock's catchy song and music video, which will guide us through the place value pattern of tens, hundreds, thousands, and beyond.

Learning Goals

I can (students will) recognize that in a multidigit whole number, a digit in one place represents ten times the value of the same digit in the place to its right, and they will apply this understanding to read and write numbers up to 1,000,000 in standard, expanded, and word forms.

I can (students will) convert numbers up to 1,000,000 between standard form, expanded form, and word form while explaining how the value of a digit changes based on its position, using patterns like "ten ones make ten" and "ten hundreds make one thousand."

Whole Brain Teaching

Play Numberock's place value song as a warm-up, and encourage your students to sing along by teaching them the chorus before they watch it: "Ten ones make ten. Ten groups of ten are one hundred. Ten hundreds make one thousand; the pattern never ends." Doing this will help reinforce the base-ten pattern you are about to teach and will remind students how place values grow by factors of ten; in the meantime, they're having fun.

Lesson: Place Value to the Millions

Duration: 15–20 minutes

VIP Vocabulary (1–2 minutes)

- Place Value: The value of a digit based on its position
- Digit: Any number 0–9
- Standard Form: The common way with digits and commas
- Word Form: Writing the number's name in words, rather than digits
- Expanded Form: Stretching the number out by place value

Digit Values

Every digit in a number has a job based on where it's placed in the number. Each period of three values is separated by a comma. Place values go on infinitely!

- Do: Write "7,268,053" on the board.
- Ask: "What place values do you already know about? What do you think the commas represent?"
- Say: "Today we're going to learn the names of all of these place values. We'll also learn to read, write, and break down numbers like this in three ways – standard, word, and expanded form."

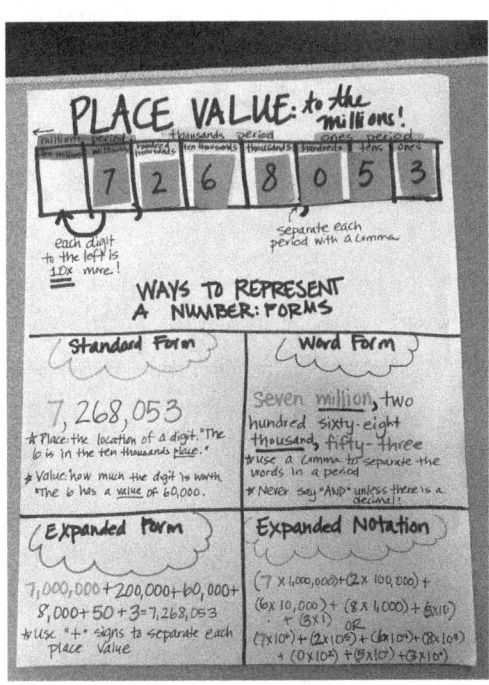

PRO TIP When making your class anchor chart, use sticky notes for the numbers on the place value chart so you can move them around and switch them out for different questions and examples!

Watch me teach it here:

Let's Rock!

Now's a great time to play Numberock's "Place Value to the Millions" song!

Place Value Song For Kids | Up To The Millions|

Place Value to the Millions	
https://numberock.com/mttm/	

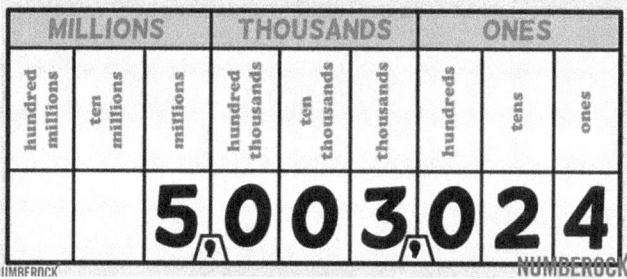

Questions Before, During, and After the Song

Before: What do you think happens to a number's value when we move a digit one place to the left?

During: Pause at 01:17, at the lyrics "Ten hundred thousands make one million." Ask, "What's the pattern between hundreds, thousands, and millions?"

After: "How would you explain to a friend why the 5 in 50,000 is worth ten times more than the 5 in 5,000?" Have your students pair up. Have one student explain, and have the other report their partner's explanation to the class.

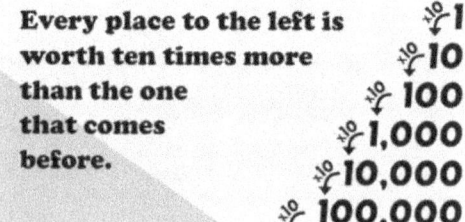

Reading and Writing Numbers

"Now that we understand the names and values of numbers to a million, let's explore different ways to represent a number."

Let's practice all three forms with our number: 7,268,053

- Standard Form: 7,268,053
  - Ask: "Why do zeros play such a big role in numbers? What happens if we forget them?"
- Word Form: Seven million, two hundred sixty-eight thousand, fifty-three
  - Ask: "What do the commas represent in the number?"
- Expanded Form: 7,000,000 + 200,000 + 60,000 + 8,000 + 50 + 3
  - Say: "We can also represent expanded form with expanded notation like this: $(7 \times 1,000,000) + (2 \times 100,000) + (6 \times 10,000) + (8 \times 1,000) + (5 \times 10) + (3 \times 1)$." ENRICH: Include expanded notation with powers of 10.
  - Ask: "When writing a number in expanded form, what happens when a digit has a value of zero?"

Partner Practice: "Write 3,205,308 in word and expanded form. Swap answers and check your partner's thinking."

Connect It!

"Numbers to the millions are everywhere – where do you spy some?"

- Example 1: The distance to the Sun is approximately 93 million miles (150 million kilometers).
- Example 2: A famous video game sold 2,500,000 copies.
- Other examples include money, population of cities, construction projects, the weight/mass of objects, and the number of online views of Numberock videos.

Team Talk: "Discuss places where you've seen a number with values in the millions or beyond." Have students share, and don't forget to add their responses to your anchor chart!

Hands-On Activity: Human Number Line

Duration: 5-10 minutes

Materials

- Large index cards (one for each student)
- Rope or tape to create a number line on the ground
- Markers or chalk (if outdoors)

Intro

"Today you'll be identifying and understanding place value by arranging yourselves in order on a human number line and answering questions about your number."

Preparation

1. Create Number Cards: Write different numbers, up to the millions, on index cards, one number on each card. On some cards, write a number in standard form; on others, in word form; on others, in expanded form; on others, in expanded notation.

2. Set Up Number Line: Use rope or tape to create an open number line on the ground, marking intervals.

Activity Steps

1. Distribute Number Cards (1 minute).

   - Arrange the Number Line (4-5 minutes).
     - Let students discuss what the intervals of the number line should be, based on the value of their assigned numbers.
     - Ask students to arrange themselves in order along the number line based on their numbers.

   - Place Value Challenges (3-4 minutes)
     - Ask a series of questions about place value and have students step forward or hold up their card when a clue about their number is called.
     - Whose number has a (choose any digit) in the thousands/hundreds/millions place? How much is it worth?
     - Tell your neighbor the expanded form of your number.
     - Find someone on the number line who has the same digit as you. How do the values of your digits compare? (For example, a 5 in the ones place versus a 5 in the hundreds place).
     - How did you know how to arrange yourselves?

Guided Practice

1. "Look at the number 4,500. What is the value of the 4? How does it change if we move it one place to the left to make 45,000?"

   Step 1: "Identify the place of the 4 in 4,500. Write 4,500 as 4 thousands plus 5 hundreds. The 4 is in the thousands place, so its value is 4,000."

   Step 2: "Move the 4 one place to the left to make 45,000. Write 45,000 as 4 ten thousands plus 5 thousands. Now that the 4 is in the ten thousands place, its value is 40,000."

   Step 3: Remind your students of the lyrics "Ten thousands make ten thousand," and remind them that the pattern grows by multiples of ten every time a number moves one place value to the left; therefore, from 4,000 to 40,000, the value increases 10 times.

2. "Write 670 in expanded form and word form."

   Step 1: "Identify the place of each digit in 670. Write 670 as 6 hundreds, 7 tens, and 0 ones. The 6 is in the hundreds place, the 7 is in the tens place, and the 0 is in the ones place."

   Step 2: "Write 670 in expanded form as 600 + 70 + 0. Since adding zero does not change the value, we can simplify it to 600 + 70."

   Step 3: "Write 670 in word form as six hundred seventy. Remind students that we do not use the word 'and' when writing whole numbers in standard word form."

3. "If 9 ones make 9, what do 9 tens make? What do 9 hundreds make?"

   Step 1: "Begin with 9 ones, which equal 9. Then move the 9 one place to the left into the tens place. Each move to the left makes the value ten times greater."

   Step 2: "Now that the 9 is in the tens place, it represents 9 tens, which equal 90."

   Step 3: "Move the 9 one more place to the left into the hundreds place. Each place to the left increases the value by 10 times again, so 9 hundreds equal 900."

   Step 4: "Remind your students that this pattern continues every time a number moves one place to the left; the value becomes ten times greater."

Practice Questions

Name/Date _____

Fill in the Blanks

1. The 7 in 7,000 is worth _____ times more than the 7 in 700.

2. Write 82,400 in expanded form: _____ + _____ + _____ .

3. Fill in the word form: 305,000 = Three hundred _____ thousand.

Multiple Choice

1. In the number 5,550, how many times greater is the value of the 5 in the thousands place than the 5 in the hundreds place?

   A. 1 time

   B. 10 times

   C. 100 times

   D. 1,000 times

2. In the song, Rob picks 9 blueberries, and one more makes 10. In the number 90, how many times greater is the 9 in the tens place than it would be in the ones place?

   A. 5 times

   B. 10 times

   C. 90 times

   D. 100 times

3. In the number 7,777, what is the relationship between the value of the 7 in the hundreds place and the 7 in the tens place?

   A. The 7 in the hundreds place is 10 times greater than the 7 in the tens place.

   B. The 7 in the hundreds place is 100 times greater than the 7 in the tens place.

   C. The 7 in the tens place is 10 times greater than the 7 in the hundreds place.

   D. The 7 in the hundreds place is the same value as the 7 in the tens place.

Short Answer

1. Explain why the 2 in 20,000 is ten times greater than the 2 in 2,000.

   _____

   _____

   _____

2. Write 450,900 in expanded form and word form.

   _____

   _____

   _____

3. How many tens are in 1,000? How many hundreds?

   _____

   _____

   _____

Open Response

Blueberry Challenge: Rob picks 6,000 blueberries. If he moves the 6 one place to the right to make 600, how many times smaller is the new number? Write a short story explaining what happened that made his blueberries go from 6,000 to 600.

   _____

   _____

   _____

   _____

   _____

Exit Ticket

1. Write 78,000 in expanded form and explain why the 7 is worth ten times more than the 7 in 7,800.

   _____

   _____

   _____

2. If 10 hundreds make 1,000, what do 10 thousands make? Explain how you know.

   _____

   _____

   _____

Notes from the Classroom

I keenly remembered as a student how daunting math was for me. So, as a math teacher I was especially careful to make sure that all students grasped the material, and I made it as fun as possible while doing it.

If a lesson was going to be particularly hard, that day I would dress all in black, and wear a 1950s hat with netting over my face. I would tell the students that I was mourning for them as the lesson was so hard, I did not know if they were going to survive it. They would always step up to the challenge to prove me wrong and inevitably would say, "That was really not that hard" as they left the classroom. They loved proving me wrong!

–Lisa Arnett

Section 2: Comparing and Ordering Numbers

Now it's time to go on a deep dive into the swampy waters of comparing and ordering numbers, where a hungry alligator will guide us through the concepts of greater than, less than, and equal to. With Numberock's "Less Than, Greater Than" song and our friend Slater the very hungry alligator, students will practice ordering numbers up to one million by comparing their digits from left to right.

Learning Goals

I can (students will) compare and order whole numbers up to 1,000,000 by analyzing place values and recording their results using the symbols <, >, and =.

Teacher Tip

Before the lesson, teach your students the chorus so they can sing along with the lyrics, "The hungry alligator eats the number that is greater. The number that is least is never part of his feast!" This will help remind students that the open side of the symbol always faces the larger number.

Whole Brain Learning

Integrate whole brain learning by pairing movements with the lyrics. For this song, try to get your students to get their arms snapping like alligator jaws to make the song more memorable and supersize their engagement.

Lesson: Comparing Place Value to the Millions

Duration: 15–20 minutes

Intro

Every number has a place – like a house on a street. We've got ones, tens, hundreds, thousands, ten thousands, hundred thousands, and millions! Today, we're going to apply what we know about smaller numbers to numbers with values to the millions. We'll figure out where they belong on the number line and how to compare them by their value based on their order.

VIP Vocabulary

Place Value: The value of a digit based on its position within a number

Digit: A single number (0–9)

Compare: Deciding which number is greater, less than, or equal to, based on its value (>, <, =)

Order: Putting numbers from least to greatest or greatest to least

---

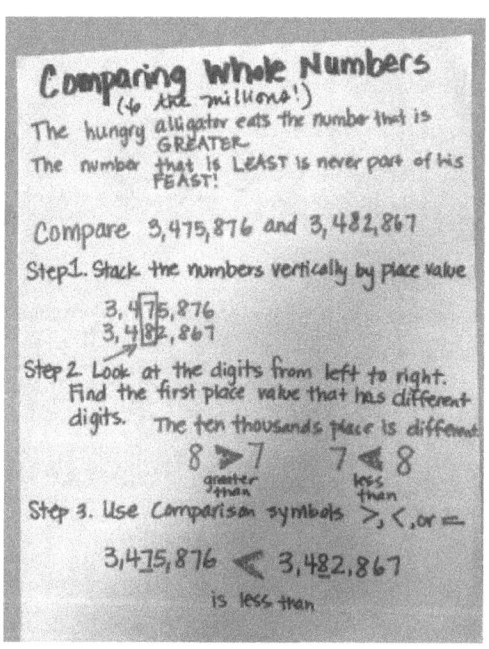

Watch me teach it here:

PRO TIP Even older kids benefit from drawing the alligator teeth on the comparison symbol to see which number the alligator "chomps."

Do: Write 3 three-digit numbers on the board (ask students to contribute).

Hundreds	Tens	Ones

- Ask: "How do you know where each of these numbers goes on a number line? How do you know which one comes first?"

Plotting and Ordering on a Number Line

Millions	Hundred Thousands	Ten Thousands	Thousands	Hundreds	Tens	Ones
6,	3	6	2,	9	8	7

- Do: Draw an open number line.
- Ask: "How do I know where to start my number line? How do I know what each line should represent?"
- Say: "I can start my number line at 6,000,000 and end it at 7,000,000. Each tick mark can represent 100,000. The number 6,362,987 will go between 6,300,000 and 6,400,000.
- Do: Repeat with the number 6,297,769.

- Ask: "Where does this number go on the number line? Which two "hundred thousands" is it between? How does this compare to the location of the first number?"
- Say: "Remember, coming before another number on a number line means the value is less, and coming after it means the value is more."

Comparing Numbers

Millions	Hundred Thousands	Ten Thousands	Thousands	Hundreds	Tens	Ones
6,	3	6	2,	9	8	7
6,	2	9	7,	7	6	9

- Say: "Let's look at the two numbers from the example before and use our place value charts to compare them."
- Ask: "Why do we start by comparing numbers from the place furthest to the left (in this case the millions) instead of the place furthest to the right (the ones)? What would happen if we compared from the right first?"
- Do: Write 6,362,987 and 6,365,762 on another place value chart like the one above.
- Ask: "If 2 numbers have the same digits in the millions and hundred thousands places like these numbers on the board, what's the next step to figure out which is greater? Why does that step matter?"

Comparing and Ordering Three Numbers

- Do: Write 3,456,789, 3,465,789 and 3,456,798 on the board.
- Ask: "How do we order and compare 3 numbers? Is it easier to look at them digit by digit or by plotting them on a number line? Which way do you think works best, and why?"

Partner Practice: Have students plot, order, and compare the three numbers from least to greatest and greatest to least and defend their thinking.

Connect It!

"When would we have to compare and order numbers to the millions?"

- Example 1: Comparing the populations of cities
- Example 2: Comparing the number of likes or views of a song or video on social media with the number of likes or views of another song or video
- Other examples: Sports stadium attendance, animal populations, money in movies or video games, distance in space, and sales

Team Talk: "Discuss a time when you've seen a need to compare and/or order values to the millions or beyond." Have students share, and don't forget to add their responses to your anchor chart!

Hands-On Activity: Event Planning

Duration: 10-15 minutes

Materials

- Whiteboard or chalkboard
- Pencils and paper (one per student or group)

Intro

"You're going to plan a super fun event for our town! It can be holiday related, a grand opening celebration . . . the sky is the limit (but your budget isn't!)."

Activity Steps

Step 1: Give students a budget of $1,000,000 to spend on 10 different items for their party (I suggest, e.g., food, equipment rentals, electricity, music, giveaways).

Step 2: Students will assign a cost to each element and list them in order from greatest to least.

Step 3: Have students pair up to discuss their events and identify the items that are most and least expensive overall.

Step 4: Additional rules can include a requirement that no one item cost more than 1/2 of the overall budget, that the students get as close to $1,000,000 as possible, etc.

Step 5: Discuss as a class the easiest way to compare numbers with similar values (for example, stacking them on top of each other to directly compare each place value), and have students justify their choices.

Guided Practice

1. "Look at the numbers 6,250 and 6,520. Which number would the alligator eat?"

Step 1: "Compare the digits in the thousands place. Both have 6, so move to the hundreds."

Step 2: "Compare the hundreds digits. The first number has 2 hundreds, the second has 5 hundreds."

Step 3: "The alligator would eat 6,520 because 5 hundreds is greater than 2 hundreds."

2. "Compare the numbers 71,400 and 71,040. Which symbol correctly compares these numbers? Write your answer."

Step 1: "Compare the digits in the ten thousands and thousands places. Both numbers have 7 ten thousands and 1 thousand, so move to the hundreds."

Step 2: "Compare the hundreds digits. The first number has 4 hundreds, and the second has 0 hundreds."

Step 3: "Since 4 hundreds is greater than 0 hundreds, 71,400 is greater than 71,040. The correct symbol is >."

3. "Plot 45,000 and 40,500 on a number line. Which number is greater? How do you know?"

Step 1: "Locate 40,000 and 50,000 on the number line to see where these two numbers fall between them."

Step 2: "Mark 40,500 just a little past 40,000, and mark 45,000 exactly halfway between 40,000 and 50,000."

Step 3: "45,000 is farther to the right on the number line, so 45,000 is greater than 40,500."

Practice Questions

Name/Date _____

Fill in the Blanks

1. In the number 345,600, the digit 4 represents _____.

2. Write the correct symbol (<, >, or =) between these numbers: 507,000 _____ 570,000.

3. The hungry alligator always eats the number that is _____.

Multiple Choice

1. What is true about the number 321,654 compared to 312,654?

   A. 321,654 < 312,654

   B. 321,654 = 312,654

   C. 321,654 > 312,654

   D. Both numbers are equal.

2. The number 780,210 is _____ 780,120.

   A. less than

   B. equal to

   C. greater than

   D. the same as

3. The digit 8 in 58,000 represents how many times more than the digit 8 in 5,800?

   A. No more than; they are the same.

   B. 10 times

   C. 100 times

   D. 1,000 times

Short Answer

1. Explain how you would compare the numbers 254,000 and 245,000.

   _____

   _____

   _____

2. Write these numbers in order from least to greatest: 812,000; 821,000; 802,000.

   _____

   _____

   _____

3. How do you know that 990,000 is greater than 909,000?

   _____

   _____

   _____

Open Response

Imagine you're a very, very hungry alligator choosing between 30,000 fish and 3,000 fish for dinner. Write a short story explaining how you decided which number of fish to eat and why the number you picked is the greater number.

_____

_____

_____

_____

_____

Exit Ticket

1. Use the correct symbol (<, >, or =) to compare these numbers: 42,000 _____ 24,000. Explain why the alligator faces the number it does.

_____

_____

_____

2. On a number line, which number would appear further to the right: 560,000 or 506,000? Explain your reasoning clearly.

_____

_____

_____

Notes from the Classroom

My first year teaching, I had a group of students who were really into giving nicknames. They just had a nickname for everyone and everything!

One student, in particular, always talked about her dad. I had never met him, not at open house, conferences, or field trips, until the very last day of school.

All year long, she referred to her dad as "Milk Dud," because, in her words, his head was shiny, smooth, and chocolatey like the candy.

So when I finally met him, shook his hand, and opened my mouth to say hello. . . do you think I called him by his name? If you guessed yes, you'd be wrong. If you guessed that I said, "Hi, Milk Dud! I'm Ms. B. It was wonderful having your daughter this year. Hope you have a great summer!" you would be absolutely right.

There is truly no bigger embarrassment than calling a parent by their child's nickname for them on the last day of school. I laugh about it now, but, oh man . . . at the time, I wanted to melt into the floor!

–Leah Brzeczkowski

Section 3: Rounding Whole Numbers

Are you ready to rock the world of rounding?! In this section, we'll discover how rounding whole numbers makes counting large amounts simpler and quicker. With a little practice, we'll be turning huge numbers into approximate amounts that are easy to count. With Numberock's catchy tune guiding us, you'll soon become rounding rock stars; so come along on an adventure to discover when to "round up" or "round down." Let's round some numbers!

Learning Goals

I can (students will) round multidigit whole numbers up to the millions place and apply the rules of rounding, recognizing when to round numbers up or down.

Teacher Tip

Use Numberock's song to reinforce rounding rules. Prior to the song, teach your students the lyrics: "If the digit's five or more, then round up. If the digit's less than five, then round down. That's how the rounded number is found!"

Whole Brain Learning

Boost whole brain learning by encouraging students to use hand gestures throughout the song: thumbs-up when rounding up and thumbs-down when rounding down. This dance move will add a kinesthetic element to the song and help students remember the lesson.

Lesson: Rounding Whole Numbers to the Millions

Duration: 15–20 minutes

Intro

Rounding means finding the closest **estimate**, which is always a multiple of 10. When rounding to a certain place value, look at the number to its right to decide whether to round up or down.

VIP Vocabulary

- Place Value: Where a digit lives in a number (like the millions or hundred thousands spot)
- Rounding: Changing a number to the nearest big, easy number (like 1,000,000) that is a multiple of 10
- Digit: A single number (0–9) in a place
- Estimate: An approximate amount that is reasonable for representing the original number
- Say: "Today, we're going to learn how to round whole numbers to the nearest million. This skill helps us simplify big numbers and make them easier to work with. Imagine you are driving on a long road trip, and you're almost out of gas. There's a gas station miles behind you and one mile in front of you. Do you turn around and go back or keep going forward? Rounding can help you decide which is closer (and will hopefully help you get gas before you run out!).

Let's Rock!

Time to play Numberock's "Rounding Number Song" Video!

Rounding Number Song	
https://numberock.com/mttm/	

Questions Before, During, and After the Song

Before: "Can any of you share a time when you might need to round numbers in real life?"

During: Pause at the car-on-the-hill trick at 2:32: "How does this visual help you decide which way to round?"

After: "Why do we change numbers to zeros after the rounded digit? Why might it be helpful to represent numbers this way?" Have your students pair up. Have one student explain, and have the other report their partner's explanation to the class.

Rounding to the nearest million

- Do: Draw a number line to represent a road. Write 6,325,149 feet on the board. This is where we are on our road trip!
- Ask: "What two millions is the number between? What was the last million I passed on the drive? What would the next million be on the road?"
- Label the endpoints on the number line (6,000,000 and 7,000,000).
- Ask: "What if we needed to stop halfway? What would the midpoint be?" (6,500,000)

Team Talk: "Is the car closer to the gas station at the 6 million mark or the 7 million mark? It's closer to 6 million, because it's before the midpoint, so we can round 6,325,149 to 6,000,000."

Rounding to a place value that is not the first digit in the number

- Group Discussion: "Using the example above, discuss what would happen if the gas stations were spaced 100,000 feet apart? Which two hundred-thousands is our number between? Which one is it closer to?"

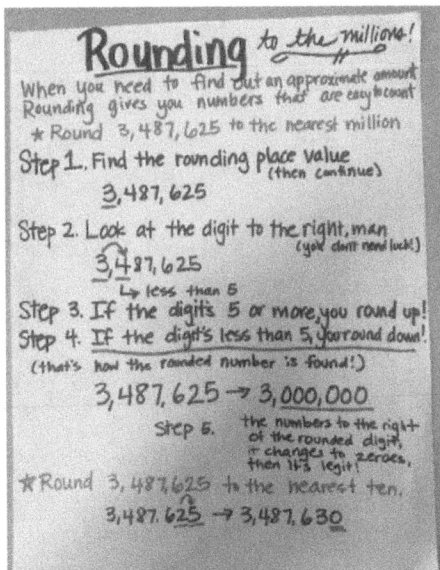

PRO TIP Remind students that estimating and rounding aren't the same thing! Rounding means we end in a multiple of 10 – it has to end in a zero – a nice ROUND number! Estimating uses a "best-guess" approach to get an approximate answer.

Watch me teach it here:

Connect It!

"Why do you think rounding numbers is useful in real life? When might we need to round a number in the millions to different place values?"

- Budgets: When people present government or corporate budgets, rounding up to the nearest million can make the figures easier to comprehend. For example, if a budget is $2,745,678, it might be rounded up to $3,000,000 for simplicity in reports and presentations.
- Population Estimates: In demographic studies, population figures are often rounded to the nearest million to provide a clear and concise overview. For instance, the population of a city with 1,234,567 inhabitants might be rounded to 1,000,000.
- Corporate Financial Reports: Companies might round up their revenue or profit figures to the nearest million in annual reports to make the data more digestible for stakeholders. For example, a revenue of $7,654,321 could be rounded up to $8,000,000.
- Space Exploration: Distances in space are often rounded up to the nearest million miles or kilometers to simplify communication. For example, the distance to a distant planet might be 123,856,789 miles, which can be rounded to 124,000,000 miles.

   Team Talk: "Are rounding and estimating the same?" Have students share, and don't forget to add their responses to your anchor chart!

Hands-On Activity: Salary Snapshot

Duration: 10–15 minutes

Intro

"Today you'll be estimating the salaries of common jobs like teacher, firefighter, and chef! Salaries can vary from place to place, so rounding can make comparing numbers easier."

Materials

- Index cards (one for each student)
- Pencil and paper to record rounding answers

Activity Steps

1. As a class, discuss jobs students might want to explore as adults and their best guess on the starting salary for that profession. Encourage students to be specific (e.g., a chef makes $36,785 per year). Give each student an index card, and have them write the profession and salary on one side.
2. On the back, have them round the number to the nearest ten thousand and the nearest thousand.
3. Split the paper into 3 columns. In the first column, students will record the profession and original salary. In the second column, they will round the salary to the nearest ten thousand. In the third column, they will round the salary to the nearest thousand.
4. Have students circulate and pair with classmates to discuss their jobs. Students will record their partner's job and the two rounded values. Their partners will then flip their cards over to check answers. Repeat the process with multiple partners until time is up.

5. Whole Group Roundup: "This rounded number helps someone quickly compare one profession's salary to the salaries of other jobs." Reinforce that rounding salaries helps people plan budgets or decide on jobs without worrying about exact cents.
6. Ask: "Why might rounding help someone choosing a job?" (e.g., "To compare salaries easily.")

Sample Salaries and Answers

- Teacher: $48,765 → $50,000 (ten thousand)
- Doctor: $208,943 → $200,000 (hundred thousand)
- Chef: $55,321 → $60,000 (ten thousand)
- Software Engineer: $132,678 → $130,000 (hundred thousand)
- Librarian: $62,456 → $60,000 (ten thousand)
- Pilot: $156,789 → $200,000 (hundred thousand)

Guided Practice

1. "Round 356,842 to the nearest thousand."

   Step 1: "Identify the digit in the thousands place: 6 (in 356,842)."
   Step 2: "Look at the digit to the right (hundreds place): 8."
   Step 3: "Since 8 is greater than or equal to 5, round up."
   Step 4: "Add 1 to the thousands digit: 6 becomes 7."
   Step 5: "Replace all digits to the right with zeros: 357,000."

2. "Round 7,492,118 to the nearest hundred thousand."

   Step 1: "Identify the digit in the hundred thousands place: 4 (in 7,492,118)."
   Step 2: "Look at the digit to the right (ten thousands place): 9."
   Step 3: "Since 9 is greater than or equal to 5, round up."
   Step 4: "Add 1 to the hundred thousands digit: 4 becomes 5."
   Step 5: "Replace all digits to the right with zeros: 7,500,000."

3. "Round 2,165,487 to the nearest million."

   Step 1: "Identify the digit in the millions place: 2 (in 2,165,487)."
   Step 2: "Look at the digit to the right (hundred thousands place): 1."
   Step 3: "Since 1 is less than 5, keep the millions digit the same."
   Step 4: "Replace all digits to the right with zeros: 2,000,000."

Practice Questions

Name/Date _____

Fill in the Blanks

1. Round 65,432 to the nearest thousand: _____

2. Round 845,627 to the nearest ten thousand: _____

3. Round 4,312,987 to the nearest hundred thousand: _____

Multiple Choice

1. What is 842,197 rounded to the nearest ten thousand?

   A. 840,000   C. 850,000

   B. 842,000   D. 800,000

2. Which number is 47,682 rounded to the nearest thousand?

   A. 47,000   C. 48,000

   B. 47,700   D. 46,000

3. Which number is 98,765 rounded to the nearest ten thousand?

   A. 90,000   C. 100,000

   B. 99,000   D. 98,000

Short Answer

1. Explain why 589,654 rounded to the nearest thousand is 590,000.

    _____

    _____

    _____

2. Round the number 9,876,543 to the nearest million and explain your reasoning.

    _____

    _____

    _____

3. Round 453,829 to the nearest ten thousand, and explain how you used place value to make your decision.

    _____

    _____

    _____

Open Response

Imagine you are in charge of hosting a school dance party that 3 classes will be attending. One class has 23 students, another has 28, and the third has 32. Use rounding to the nearest ten to estimate how many students will attend in all. Why might rounding like this be useful for planning food, seating, and supplies?

_____

_____

_____

_____

_____

Exit Ticket

1. Round 3,465,321 to the nearest ten thousand and explain your reasoning.

    _____

    _____

    _____

2. Why is rounding helpful when dealing with very large numbers?

    _____

    _____

    _____

02 Computation with Whole Numbers

Notes from the Classroom

At the beginning of the year, I used a test with story problems to help determine students' math ability levels. Here is a problem with the student's actual answer.

If Susan was born in 1970, how old would she be in 2035?

There was quite a bit of figuring on the paper, which was erased before this answer was given: "Ded probly."

–Marlene Ross

Section 1: Adding and Subtracting Whole Numbers

In this lesson, we'll dive into adding and subtracting multidigit whole numbers using the standard algorithm—with regrouping when necessary! We'll bring these skills to life through two Numberock songs: "Addition with Regrouping" and "Subtraction with Regrouping." Plus, students will practice checking their work with the inverse operation—a powerful strategy for preparing to take a test.

Learning Goals

I can (students will) fluently add and subtract multidigit whole numbers using the standard algorithm, regrouping when necessary, to solve real-world problems.

Teacher Tip

Regrouping can be confusing if students think it's just "moving a number." Instead, use base-ten blocks to model regrouping clearly: show that when digits are "carried" or "borrowed," you're really trading ten smaller units for one larger one (or vice versa). Connect these models to the standard algorithm visually, so students see how the "carrying" and "borrowing" in the traditional method match the underlying math.

Whole Brain Teaching

In the "Addition with Regrouping" song, teach students the chorus line:
"We mathematicians add with precision, regrouping tens and hundreds when we find double digits in addition." Have them strike a "disco" pose (finger pointed up) every time they regroup, showing how tens separate from ones.

Lesson: Addition and Subtraction Within 1,000,000

Duration: 15–20 minutes

Intro

"Adding and subtracting with larger numbers requires us to stay organized and have solid place value understanding and number sense. It's a great idea to practice estimating before doing the actual calculations to check for accuracy!"

VIP Vocabulary

- Sum: The answer to an addition problem
- Difference: The answer to a subtraction problem
- Place Value: The value of a digit based on its position
- Regrouping: Process of making groups of tens when carrying out operations like addition and subtraction with two-digit numbers or larger

---

- Do: Write 214,506 + 86,347 and 72,153 − 9,684
- Ask: "Why do you think we need to line up numbers by place value before adding or subtracting? What would happen if we didn't line them up by place value?"
- Say: "Today, we're learning to add and subtract numbers up to the millions by lining up their place values. Then, we add or subtract from right to left, regrouping when needed."

Addition with Regrouping

A place value chart is a great starting place for addition with regrouping, especially when you're dealing with larger numbers. I like to use the place value mat below for students who need a tactile way to regroup ones into tens, tens into hundreds, etc. Use small counters with the number "1" written on them so students can move them over to the next place value when needed.

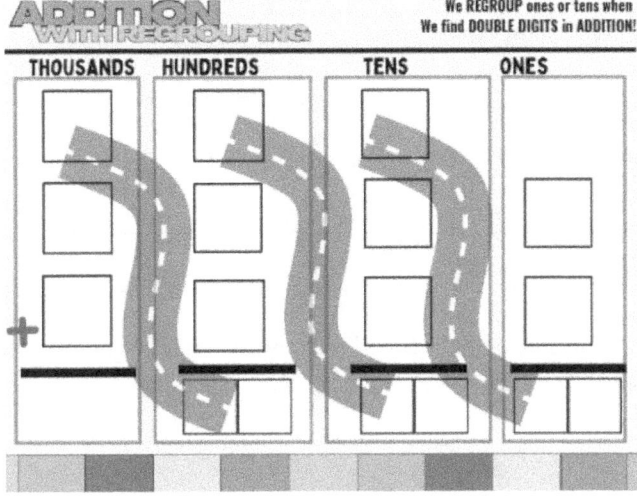

Let's Rock!

Time to play Numberock's "Addition with Regrouping" song!

Addition with Regrouping	
https://numberock.com/mttm/	

Questions Before, During, and After the Song

Before: "If we add two numbers like 15 and 26, and get 11 when adding the ones, what happens to the extra ten? Where does it go?"

During: Pause at 1:06, at the lyrics "regrouping tens and hundreds when we find double digits in addition." Ask: "Why does this regrouping happen? How does number sense explain it?"

After: "Could we use the same regrouping strategy at the thousands place or even higher? How is it the same as regrouping tens and hundreds?"

Watch me teach it here:

Let's Practice!

- Say: "A zoo tracks visitors. Last year, 214,506 people visited, and this year 86,347 came. How many visitors came to the zoo in both years combined?"
- Do: Draw the place value charts on the board. Have students help fill in each place value name.

Hundred thousands	Ten thousands	Thousands	Hundreds	Tens	Ones

- Choose 2 students to come to the board and decide where each number belongs on the place value chart.

- Ask: "Which place values will have to be regrouped? How do you know?"

Hundred thousands	Ten thousands	Thousands	Hundreds	Tens	Ones
1	1			1	
2	1	4,	5	0	6
	8	6,	3	4	7
sum: 3	10	10	8	5	13

The sum of 214,506 and 86,347 is 300,853.

ADDITION WITH REGROUPING
WE REGROUP PLACE VALUES WHEN,
WE SEE DOUBLE DIGITS IN ADDITION!!

PRO TIP Using the lyrics "We regroup place values when we see double digits in addition" and repeating them when you solve an addition problem with regrouping is a great way for students to reinforce the concept!

Subtraction with Regrouping

Watch me teach it here:

Subtracting with multiple steps of regrouping, particularly subtracting across zeroes, can sometimes be tricky, even for our strongest mathematicians! The idea is to go slow and steady, taking one place value at a time, as if they were separate problems. In this section, I'll show you my favorite math hack – using compensation to subtract across zeros to eliminate regrouping!

Let's Rock!

Time to play Numberock's "Subtraction with Regrouping" song!

Subtraction with Regrouping	
https://numberock.com/mttm/	

Questions Before, During, and After the Song

Before: "If we subtract 20 – 12 and start with the ones, why might we run into a problem? What would we need to do?"

During: Pause at 0:48, at the lyrics "We regroup a ten into ten ones when the top number's smaller." Ask: "How is it possible to solve 0 – 1 after regrouping?"

After: "How would you regroup if you needed to borrow in the thousands place or ten thousands place? What would stay the same about the regrouping process?"

Let's Practice!

- Say: "Let's use our zoo example from above: Last year, 214,506 people visited, and this year 86,347 came. How many more visitors came to the zoo last year than this year?"

Hundred thousands	Ten thousands	Thousands	Hundreds	Tens	Ones
2	1	4,	⑤	⓪	⑥
	8	6,	3	4	⑦
difference:					

- Do: Circle the digits in the one's place.
- Ask: Can 6 minus 7 be done? NO! Because the top number's smaller than the bottom one. SO, we regroup a ten into ten ones when the top number's small in subtraction!
- Ask: "What happens when we go to the tens place to regroup? Are any tens available? What should the next step be?"
- Do: Model regrouping from the hundreds to the tens.
- Ask: "Now that we have 10 tens, how can we regroup again to make sure we have enough ones?"

- Do: Model subtracting hundreds, tens, and ones.

Hundred thousands	Ten thousands	Thousands	Hundreds	Tens	Ones
2	1	4,	5	0	6
	8	6,	3	4	7
difference:			1	5	9

- Ask: "How can we repeat the process with the remaining place values? Which ones will need to be regrouped? How do you know?"

Hundred thousands	Ten thousands	Thousands	Hundreds	Tens	Ones
2	1	4,	5	0	6
	8	6,	3	4	7
difference:			1	5	9

Hundred thousands	Ten thousands	Thousands	Hundreds	Tens	Ones
2	1	14,	5	0	6
	8	6,	3	4	7
difference: 1	2	8,	1	5	9

PRO TIP "We regroup a ten into ten ones when the top number's smaller in subtraction!" Have students sweep their right arm from left to right in a rainbow arc over their heads, symbolizing borrowing from a higher place value. This physical movement will help lock the regrouping concept into students' long-term memory.

Watch me teach it here:

Subtract Across Zeros Using Compensation

This strategy, called compensation, is a super easy alternative for kids (and adults!) who struggle with regrouping across multiple zeros.

When your whole number has a zero in the final place value(s), you can subtract one from both the whole and the part, and the difference between the two numbers will stay the same!

$$
\begin{array}{r}
5000 \ \ -1 \\
-1926 \ \ -1 \\
\end{array}
\qquad
\begin{array}{r}
4999 \\
-1925 \\
\hline
3074 \\
\end{array}
$$

SUBTRACTION
with Regrouping
More on the top,   3,829
no need to stop. − 634
                    ‾‾‾‾‾5

2 minus 3 can't   7 12
be done because   3,8̶2̶9
the top number's − 634
smaller the   ‾‾‾‾95
bottom one.

So we regroup   7 12
a ten into ten   3,8̶2̶9
ones, when the−   634
top number's   ‾‾‾‾‾‾
smaller in   3,195
subtraction.

Watch me teach it here:

Connect It!

"Can you think of a real-world situation where you'd need to add or subtract numbers this big? How would you use the answer?"

- Example 1: Budgets for big businesses and government spending
- Example 2: Populations of major towns and cities
- Other examples: Salaries, construction projects, distances between faraway locations, housing costs, and views/likes on social media content

Team Talk: "Discuss places where you've seen addition or subtraction with values up to the millions (or beyond)." Have students share, and don't forget to add their responses to your anchor chart!

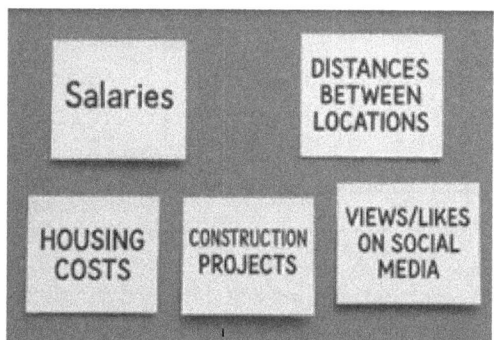

Hands-On Activity: Planting a School-Wide Garden

Duration: 10–15 minutes

Materials

- Poster board or card stock for each student/team
- Markers or chalk

Intro

"You've just won a million-dollar grant to beautify your school with a garden and will need to allocate funds for different items such as plants, soil, tools, and decorations."

Activity Steps

1. Setting the Budget

- Give each group a budget of $1,000,000.
- Students must purchase as many items as they can from the list below for the garden without going over budget. They may purchase as many of one item as they'd like but must have at least five different components in their budget.

2. Shopping Time! "Shop from the list below to build the garden of your school's dreams!"

- Plants: $12,956
- Soil: $34,165
- Tools: $30,272
- Decorations: $26,119
- Fencing: $89,123
- Watering System: $78,456
- Benches: $4,878

- Pathways: $67,490
- Compost Bins: $1,345
- Garden Shed: $56,009
- Mulch: $3,436
- Raised Beds: $16,567
- Greenhouse: $98,789
- Lighting: $45,123

- Bird Feeders: $9,876
- Garden Signs: $4,567
- Pest Control: $15,678
- Fertilizer: $8,234
- Rain Barrels: $11,945
- Picnic Tables: $19,476

3. Presentation and Discussion

- Each group will present their budget plan to the class.
- Discuss the different choices made by each group and how they managed their budget.

Guided Practice

1. Solve 347 + 586 using the standard algorithm.

   Step 1: Line up the numbers vertically by their place values, with the ones, tens, and hundreds digits aligned.

   Step 2: Add the ones place. 7 plus 6 equals 13. Write down the 3 in the ones place and carry the 1 to the tens place.

   Step 3: Add the tens place. 4 plus 8 equals 12, plus 1 more equals 13. Write down the 3 in the tens place and carry the 1 to the hundreds place.

   Step 4: Add the hundreds place. 3 plus 5 equals 8, plus 1 more equals 9. Write down the 9 in the hundreds place.

   Step 5: The final sum is 933.

2. Solve 742 − 398. Explain what you did when you had to regroup.

   Step 1: Line up the numbers vertically by their place values, with the ones, tens, and hundreds digits aligned.

   Step 2: Start with the ones place. You cannot subtract 8 from 2, so regroup 1 ten from the tens place. The 4 tens become 3 tens, and the 2 ones become 12 ones.

   Step 3: Now subtract the ones place. 12 minus 8 equals 4.

   Step 4: Move to the tens place. You cannot subtract 9 from 3, so regroup 1 hundred from the hundreds place. The 7 hundreds become 6 hundreds, and the 3 tens become 13 tens.

   Step 5: Subtract the tens place. 13 minus 9 equals 4.

   Step 6: Subtract the hundreds place. 6 minus 3 equals 3.

   Step 7: The final difference is 344.

3. Solve 8,549 + 7,682. How many times did you regroup in your work?

   Step 1: Line up the numbers vertically by their place values, with the ones, tens, hundreds, and thousands digits aligned.

   Step 2: Add the ones place. 9 plus 2 equals 11. Write down the 1 in the ones place and carry the 1 to the tens place.

   Step 3: Add the tens place. 4 plus 8 equals 12, plus 1 more equals 13. Write down the 3 in the tens place and carry the 1 to the hundreds place.

   Step 4: Add the hundreds place. 5 plus 6 equals 11, plus 1 more equals 12. Write down the 2 in the hundreds place and carry the 1 to the thousands place.

   Step 5: Add the thousands place. 8 plus 7 equals 15, plus 1 more equals 16. Write down the 16.

   Step 6: The final sum is 16,231. You regrouped 3 times in your work.

Practice Questions

Name/Date _____

Fill in the Blanks

1. 754 + 628 = _____

2. 913 − 475 = _____

3. When the top digit is smaller than the bottom digit in subtraction, you must

   _____.

Multiple Choice

1. When adding 267 + 458, why do you regroup?

   A. Because you run out of room

   B. Because two digits add to more than 9

   C. Because you have to borrow

   D. Because you're multiplying

2. What should you do first when subtracting 403 − 289?

   A. Add the digits

   B. Subtract ones

   C. Regroup from the tens place

   D. Regroup from the hundreds place

3. What is the best way to check your addition?

   A. Multiply by 2

   B. Add the opposite way

   C. Use subtraction (the inverse operation)

   D. Estimate the sum

Short Answer

1. Explain why we need to regroup when adding 486 + 579.

   _____

   _____

   _____

2. Solve 1,204 − 867 and describe how you regrouped.

   _____

   _____

   _____

3. When subtracting 6,002 − 2,738, explain what you must do if a place value has a 0.

   _____

   _____

   _____

Open Response

You are helping set up chairs for an assembly. There are 287 chairs on one side of the gym and 428 chairs on the other side. Write an equation to find the total number of chairs, show your work with regrouping, and explain how you know your answer is correct using the inverse operation.

_____

_____

_____

_____

_____

Exit Ticket

1. Solve $6{,}891 + 4{,}292$. Did you need to regroup? Explain why or why not.

_____

_____

_____

2. Solve $5{,}000 - 2{,}783$. Check your work with the inverse operation.

_____

_____

_____

Notes from the Classroom

One year while giving my students a math test, I had a little girl counting on her fingers but realized she didn't have enough fingers so she pulled up her foot and was using her toes by pressing on them through her sneakers! I thought this was hysterical and ingenious at the same time.

–Jen Bravo

Section 2: Multiplying Whole Numbers

Learning how to multiply up to a four-digit number by a one-digit number, or multiplying two two-digit numbers, is one of the great milestones that students achieve in fourth grade mathematics. To help build fluency, we begin with conceptual models that show how multiplication works. In the Numberock song "Multiplying by a Single Digit," we follow two kids as they buy blueberries at the store and collect cans for recycling. This song introduces the partial products method, helping students understand how multiplication can be broken down into place value steps. Later, we visit a farm in the Numberock "Area Model for Multiplication" song, where a farmer tracks rows of green beans using the area model. This combination of music, place value strategies, and visual modeling will help students not only memorize the steps for long multiplication but also understand the reasoning behind them.

Learning Goals

I can (students will) be able to multiply a one-digit number by up to a four-digit number, as well as multiply two two-digit numbers using their understanding of place value strategies and the area model of multiplication.

Teacher Tip

While it may be tempting to jump straight into the standard algorithm for long multiplication, constructivist teaching encourages students to first develop a deep understanding of what's happening behind the scenes. Using base ten blocks or drawings can support students as they visualize what multiplication means. Try modeling a small two-digit equation, like 12×13, then represent it using both the partial products strategy and area model to connect concrete understanding with abstract methods.

Whole Brain Learning

To incorporate whole brain learning into this lesson, have students use their hands to represent the place values being multiplied. When solving a problem like 34×5, students can raise four fingers and five fingers to represent the ones. Then, to represent multiplying 30 by 5, they can form a three and a zero consecutively with one hand, and then show five fingers on the other hand, and to make it more engaging, try having students face a partner whenever they do this. These kinesthetic cues help solidify the structure of multiplication in a fun and memorable way.

Lesson: Multiplying Whole Numbers

Duration: 15–20 minutes

Intro

Multiplying double- and triple-digit numbers can seem daunting for students who seemingly JUST learned to multiply and are still working on their fluency. In this section I'll share a few great strategies that will give your students the confidence they need to tackle even the scariest of problems!

VIP Vocabulary

- Factor: A number that is multiplied by another number to get a product
- Product: The result of multiplying two or more numbers
- Area Model: A visual representation of multiplication using a square model
- Partial Product: The product you get in each step of the partial product method
- Lattice Method: An alternative method to standard algorithm using diagonal partial products
- Standard Algorithm: The traditional step-by-step method for multiplying numbers

---

Do: Write the following on the board:
- 3×5
- 3×50
- 30×50
- 30×55

Ask: "How are these expressions related? How does the place value of the product change as the place values of the factors change?"

Say: "Today we're going to expand our knowledge of multiplication to include multidigit numbers. We're going to learn a couple of different strategies to help us solve, and you get to decide which way works best for you!"

Area Model/Partial Product

Area models are a version of the model students learned in third grade for the distributive property. Partial products are the smaller products in each part of the model. Students can transition to partial products without the area model when they have mastered using the rectangle for support.

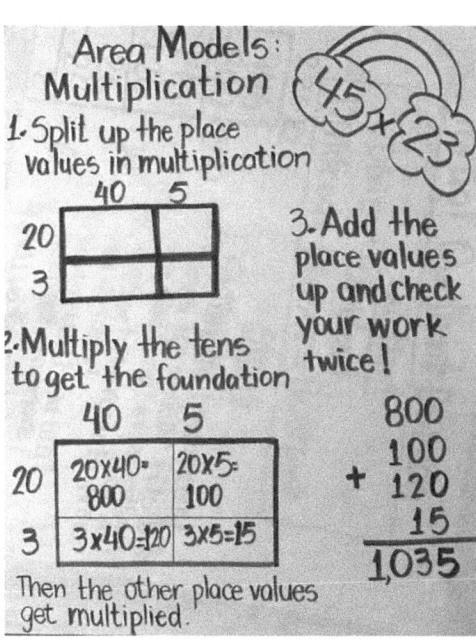

PRO TIP Identify the number of partial products in the problem by multiplying the number of digits in each factor. For example, a 2-digit by 2-digit number will have 4 partial products because 2 × 2 = 4!

Let's Rock!

Time to play Numberock's "Area Model" song!

Area Model	
https://numberock.com/mttm/	

Questions Before, During, and After the Song

Before: If you can multiply 4 × 5, what is the product? Now try 30 × 5. What is the product? Do you think solving these simpler problems could help solve 34 × 5? How might you break the number apart to solve it?

During: After verse two, pause and ask: How did we get to the partial products of 10, 20, 100, and 200? Why do we add these numbers together after we find them?

After: How did the song help you understand how to multiply larger numbers? Do you find the partial products method or the area model more helpful in understanding how multiplication works?

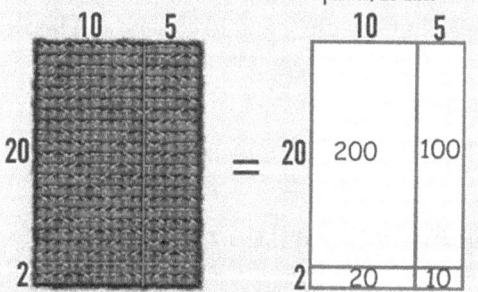

Area Model

To solve a 2-digit by 2-digit multiplication problem, first split up the place values. To find out how many bean plants are in a field that has 22 rows of 15 plants, do this:

Then, add the partial products to find the total product.

$$\begin{array}{r} 200 \\ 100 \\ 20 \\ + \quad 10 \\ \hline 330 \end{array}$$
bean plants

Let's Practice!

I use the lyrics of Numberock's "Area Model" song to walk students through each step of solving a multiplication problem using area models!

- **Do**: Write 45 × 23 on the board.
  - Step 1: Split up the place values in multiplication.
  - Step 2: Multiply the tens to get the foundation.
  - Step 3: Then the other place values get multiplied.
  - Step 4: Add the partial products up, and check your work twice.
- **Say:** "Why do you think breaking down the numbers into smaller parts helps in solving multiplication problems?"
- **Enrichment:** When students are ready, have them try to remove the model for support and write the partial products on their own. Remember to use the Pro Tip above to identify how many partial products are needed for each problem.

Lattice Method

Watch me teach it here:

Based on Italian and Chinese multiplication strategies, the lattice method is (in my opinion) an undertaught strategy, particularly for kids who are still building their number sense and need a more streamlined option!

Just like with area models, have students draw a grid with as many rows and columns as the digits in the numbers they're multiplying. For example, if you're multiplying 42 by 65, you'll need a 2 × 2 grid because each number has two digits.

Step 1: Label the Grid: Write one number along the top of the grid and the other number along the right side. For 42 × 65, write 4 and 2 along the top and 6 and 5 along the right side (this is slightly different from the area model method because the number is not broken into place VALUES, just into digits).

Step 2: Diagonals: Draw diagonal lines through each box in the grid, from the top right corner to the bottom left corner. These lines will help you organize your partial products.

Step 3: Multiply and Fill In: Multiply the digits at the top and side of each box and write the product in the corresponding box. If the product is a two-digit number, write the tens digit above the diagonal and the ones digit below the diagonal.

Step 4: Add Along the Diagonals: Add the numbers along each diagonal, starting from the bottom right corner. Write the sums outside the grid along the bottom and left sides.

Step 5: Combine the Sums: Combine the sums from the diagonals to get the final product. If any diagonal sum is a two-digit number, carry over the tens digit to the next diagonal.

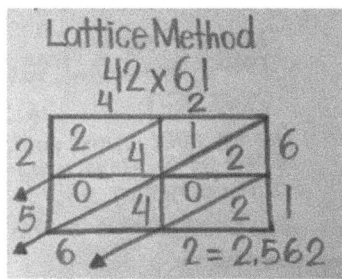

Standard Algorithm

As your students build understanding of the "why" behind the place values of multidigit multiplication, they can navigate to standard algorithm to solve multidigit multiplication problems more efficiently!

Do: Write 59 × 25 on the board.

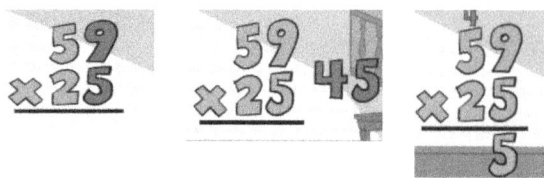

- Step 1: Multiply the ones place times the ones place. Regroup double-digit products to the tens place.
- Step 2: Multiply the ones times the tens. Don't forget to add the regrouping!

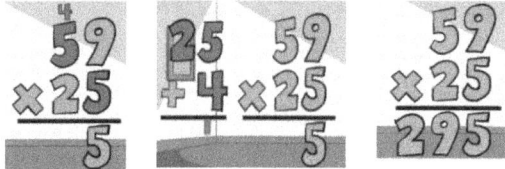

- Step 3: Drop a zero before starting with the tens place!
- Step 4: Multiply the tens place times the ones place. **Regroup double-digit products to the tens place.**

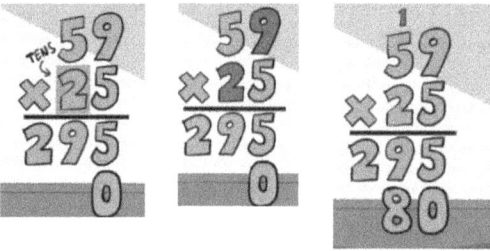

- Step 5: Multiply the tens times the tens. Don't forget to add the regrouping!

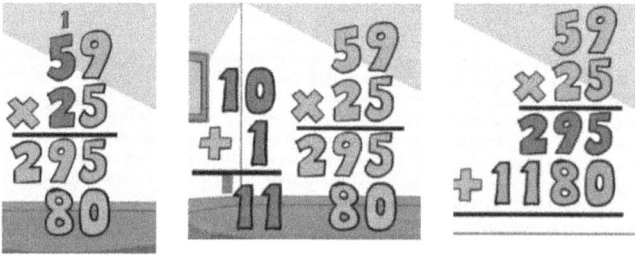

- Step 6: Add the two partial products together to find the sum!

HOT Question: "How does the standard algorithm ensure that all parts of the multiplication problem are accounted for? What would happen if we missed a step?"

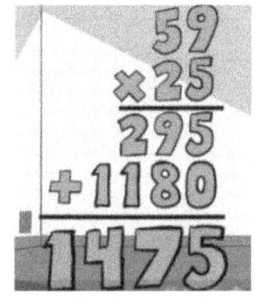

Partner Practice: "If each row of your garden has 23 plants and there are 15 rows, how many plants are there in total? Use the area model, partial product, and standard algorithm to solve it."

HOT Question: "How can understanding different multiplication strategies help you solve real-world problems more effectively? Can you think of another real-world example where you might use multiplication?"

Connect It!

"Can you think of a real-world situation where you'd need to multiply multidigit numbers? How would you use the answer?"

- Example 1: Anything that involves finding the area – planting a garden, laying tile, painting walls, etc.
- Example 2: Ordering and inventory of large companies
- Other examples: Budgeting, cooking/baking multiple servings, shopping, travel, real estate, and more

Team Talk: "Discuss places where you've seen multidigit multiplication in the real world." (Have students share, and don't forget to add their responses to your anchor chart!)

Hands-On Activity: Garden Supply Shop

Duration: 10-15 minutes

Materials

- Whiteboard
- Pencils and paper
- Timer

Intro

"You're planners for a community garden! To save money, you're going to a garden supply warehouse to buy in bulk. Each set of items must be purchased in the quantity listed to receive the discounted price. You'll multiply big numbers to figure out how much supplies cost – like seed packets and shovels – to stay on budget."

Activity Steps

1. Setting the Budget
   - Give each group a budget of $10,000.
   - Remember, items on the list have to be purchased by the quantity listed. Students may purchase as many sets of items as they'd like as long as they stay within their budget.

2. "Shopping Time! Use the list below to go shopping from the garden supply warehouse. Calculate the price of each set of items before checking out. Make sure you get all the items you need to plant a garden successfully!"

   - Seed Packets: $24 per packet. Minimum Quantity: 35 packets
   - Bird Feeders: $9 per feeder. Minimum Quantity: 95 feeders
   - Mulch: $34 per bag. Minimum Quantity: 30 bags
   - Shovels: $18 per shovel. Minimum Quantity: 42 shovels
   - Fence Posts: $15 per post. Minimum Quantity: 63 posts
   - Soil: $27 per bag. Minimum Quantity: 14 bags
   - Fertilizer: $36 per bag. Minimum Quantity: 28 bags
   - Garden Signs: $8 per sign. Minimum Quantity: 132 signs
   - Sprinklers: $39 per sprinkler. Minimum Quantity: 24 sprinklers
   - Flower Bulbs: $12 per bulb. Minimum Quantity: 68 bulbs
   - Compost Bins: $88 per bin. Minimum Quantity: 12 bins
   - Garden Shed: $250 per shed. Minimum Quantity: 5 sheds
   - Raised Beds: $16 per bed. Minimum Quantity: 22 beds
   - Greenhouse: $987. Minimum Quantity: 3 greenhouses
   - Lighting: $45 per box of lights. Minimum Quantity: 19 boxes

3. Presentation and Discussion

- Each group will present their plan to the class.
- Discuss the different choices made by each group and how they managed their budget.

Guided Practice

1. Solve 34 × 5 using partial products.

   Step 1: Multiply 30 × 5 = 150.
   Step 2: Multiply 4 × 5 = 20.
   Step 3: Add the partial products: 150 + 20 = 170.

2. Solve 28 × 9 using partial products.

   Step 1: Break apart 28 into 20 and 8.
   Step 2: Multiply 20 × 9 = 180.
   Step 3: Multiply 8 × 9 = 72.
   Step 4: Add the partial products: 180 + 72 = 252.
   Step 5: The final product is 252.

3. Solve 42 × 60 using partial products.

   Step 1: Break apart 42 into 40 and 2.
   Step 2: Multiply 40 × 60 = 2,400.
   Step 3: Multiply 2 × 60 = 120.
   Step 4: Add the partial products: 2,400 + 120 = 2,520.
   Step 5: The final product is 2,520.

Practice Problems

Name/Date _____

Fill in the Blanks

1. When using partial products, you multiply each _____ separately.

2. The product of 30 × 4 is _____.

3. To find the final product, you must _____ the partial products.

Multiple Choice

1. What is the product of 43 × 2?

   A. 76   C. 96

   B. 86   D. 106

2. What is 27 × 3 using partial products?

   A. 80   C. 60 + 27 = 87

   B. 60 + 21 = 81   D. 70 + 27 = 97

3. What is 46 × 43?

   A. 1,643   C. 1,946

   B. 1,978   D. 2,047

Short Answer

1. Why is it helpful to break numbers apart by place value when multiplying?

   _____

   _____

   _____

2. A farmer plants 12 rows of carrots with 15 carrots in each row. How many carrots does he plant in all?

   _____

   _____

   _____

3. Jamie collected 28 bags of cans. Each bag holds 19 cans. How many cans did Jamie collect in total? Use partial products to solve.

   _____

   _____

   _____

Open Response

Two kids each buy 23 trays of blueberries. Each tray has 15 blueberries. Using the partial products method, figure out how many blueberries they bought in total. Show your work and explain why this strategy helps you understand the multiplication.

_____

_____

_____

_____

_____

Exit Ticket

1. Solve 53 × 6 using partial products. Show each step.

   _____

   _____

   _____

2. Two friends collected cans for a school fundraiser. One collected 32 bags, and the other collected 25 bags. If each bag has 8 cans, how many cans did they collect altogether? Show your work.

   _____

   _____

   _____

Notes from the Classroom

My building is directly across the street from our central administration building. When our central administration comes to do a walk-through (informal observation) I usually know they are on the move because I can see them. Well, they came this week. My students were transitioning from fluency warm-up to whole-group lesson and were putting something away, when they spotted them. Suddenly I hear, "MS. MAC, MS. MAC! THE SUITS ARE COMING!" Fast forward, the "suits" did come and upon them leaving the room, you could feel everyone breathe. . .. Then this 15-minute ordeal ends with, "MS. MAC–WE CRUSHED THAT!" I love these little humans, and yes, they did crush it!

–Jessica McIlhenney

Section 3: Dividing Whole Numbers by One-Digit Divisors

In this section, we are going to build on the foundational division strategies learned in third grade, such as repeated subtraction, and apply that knowledge to new methods including the partial quotient method (also known as the big 7 method) and the area model. We will also introduce the standard algorithm for division using one-digit divisors. Through Numberock's fun and engaging song, students will follow nine scuba-diving characters who discover 225 rubies and need to divide them equally. The song walks students through solving this problem using both the partial quotient method and the area model. Students will use their number sense and understanding of place value to build confidence in their division skills.

Learning Goals

I can (students will be able to) divide dividends with up to four digits by one-digit divisors using strategies based on place value and number sense.

Teacher Tip

Before introducing long division, it is helpful to review multiplying by multiples of 10. In the song, we work with the number 9. Remind students that if $9 \times 2 = 18$, then $9 \times 20 = 180$ and $9 \times 30 = 270$. This helps them estimate and subtract groups more efficiently when using the partial quotient method.

Whole Brain Teaching

To enhance retention through kinesthetic learning, use physical movements that correspond to the chorus of the song. When the lyrics say "subtract groups of the divisor," students can make a small ball with their hands. For "from the dividend," they can expand their arms into a large circle to represent the larger quantity. When the lyrics say "until there's a remainder," students make a half circle with one arm and extend their leg to form a capital *R*. Finally, for "or a zero at the end," they raise their arms above their heads and touch their fingers together to form a zero. These movements strengthen memory by anchoring math vocabulary to physical cues.

Lesson: Division with Partial Quotient

Duration: 15–20 minutes

Intro

The partial quotient strategy is a method of division that breaks down the division process into more manageable steps. It's particularly useful for students who are just learning division, as it emphasizes understanding over memorization and continues to reinforce multiplication skills and number sense. This method can be a stepping stone to more advanced division techniques like standard algorithm!

Here's a step-by-step guide to walking your student through dividing with partial quotients:

1. Estimate and Subtract
   - "Start by estimating how many times the divisor can fit into the dividend. This doesn't have to be exact; it's just a rough estimate!"
   - "Multiply the divisor by this estimate and subtract the result from the dividend. Write down the partial quotient (the estimate) on the side."

2. Repeat the Process
   - "Take the remainder from the subtraction and repeat the process: estimate how many times the divisor can fit into the new number, multiply, and subtract."
   - "Continue this process until the remainder is smaller than the divisor."

3. Add Up the Partial Quotients
   - "Once you can't divide any further, add up all the partial quotients to get the final quotient."
   - "If there's a remainder, it will be the leftover amount that couldn't be divided."

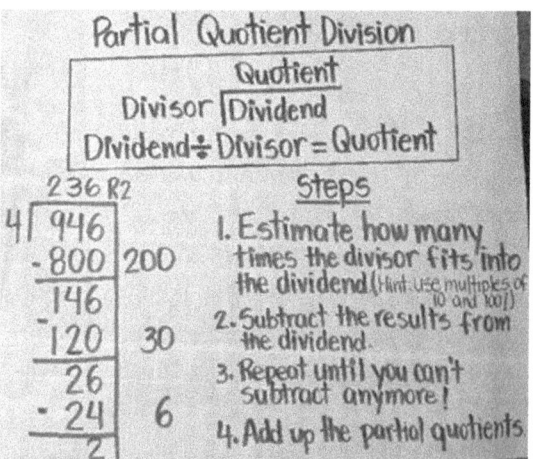

Watch me teach it here:

PRO TIP Have students write out the first 10 multiples of the divisor off to the side before beginning any division! This makes it so much easier to find partial quotients!

Let's Rock!

Time to play Numberock's "Partial Quotient" song!

Partial Quotient	
https://numberock.com/mttm/	

Questions Before, During, and After the Song

Before: "If we wanted to divide a large number in the hundreds by a one-digit number, what strategies do we already use that could help us do this?"

During: "When we divide using the partial quotient method, what do we keep track of on the right side of the division bracket, often called the Big 7?"

After: "In what ways are the partial quotient method and the area model similar? Which one makes more sense to you?"

Let's Practice!

Have students work in pairs to solve the following division problems using partial quotients!

Ask: "Your teacher has 768 pencils and needs to pack them into boxes of 8. How many boxes does she need?"

Ask: "A farmer has 4,567 apples and wants to pack them into crates of 9. How many crates does he need?" (Check out "What Remains?" for help if you get stuck!)

What Remains?

You're doing great at division but not sure what to do when there's an amount leftover? How you handle the remainder in a division problem depends on the context of the problem. Here are some common ways to deal with remainders:

1. Round Up
   - When to Use: If the problem requires a whole number and you need to ensure that everyone or everything is included.

- Example: If you have 27 students and you need to form groups of 5, you would need 6 groups (since 5 groups would cover only 25 students, and you have 2 students left over).

2. Ignore the Remainder

- When to Use: If the remainder doesn't affect the outcome or if you only need the whole number part of the quotient.
- Example: If you are dividing 27 candies among 5 children, each child would get 5 candies, and you would ignore the 2 candies left over.

3. Use the Remainder

- When to Use: If the remainder itself is important to the problem.
- Example: If you are dividing 27 apples into bags of 5, the remainder tells you that you have 2 apples left over after filling 5 bags."

Examples

1. Round Up

- Problem: "You have 27 students and need to form groups of 5."
- Solution: "(27 divided by 5 = 5) R2, so you need 6 groups to include all students."

2. Ignore the Remainder

- Problem: "You have 27 candies and want to give each child an equal amount."
- Solution: "(27 divided by 5 = 5) R2, so each child gets 5 candies."

3. Use the Remainder

- Problem: "You have 27 apples and want to know how many are left after making bags of 5."
- Solution: "(27 divided by 5 = 5) R2, so you have 2 apples left over."

Let's Practice!

"Let's try one together:"

- Problem: "You have 34 books and want to place them on shelves that hold 6 books each. How many shelves do you need, and how many books will be left over?"
  1. Divide: "(34 divided by 6 = 5) R4"

  2. Round Up: "You need 6 shelves to hold all the books."

  3. Use the Remainder: "You will have 4 books left over."

    "Would you like more practice problems or further explanations?"

Connect It!

"Why is it important to know how to divide large numbers? Can you think of other situations where you might need to use division in real life?"

- Example 1: Sharing equally: Dividing candies among friends, distributing supplies in a classroom
- Example 2: Budgeting: Dividing money for savings, expenses, and donations
- Example 3: Packing: Dividing items into boxes or crates for shipping

Team Talk: "Discuss places where you've seen long division with single-digit divisors (or beyond)." Have students share, and don't forget to add their responses to your anchor chart!

Hands-On Activity: Running a Pizza Shop

Duration: 10–15 minutes

Materials

- Pizza shop menu (printed or digital)
- Budget sheets
- Pencils and erasers
- Whiteboard and markers

Intro

"Today, you and your business partner are going to have some fun opening up a mini pizza shop! Before you can open, you'll need to solve some problems that pizza shop owners face every day. You'll figure out how much your ingredients cost, how much money you made, and how you can budget based on your sales so you can be successful business owners!"

Activity Steps

1. Setting the Menu: "Use the menu below to solve the problems in step 3!" Students can add their own pizzas and ingredients and create problems to solve as enrichment!

   Mini Pizza Shop Menu
   - Mini Cheese Pizza: $8
   - Mini Pepperoni Pizza: $7
   - Mini Veggie Pizza: $6
   - Mini Margherita Pizza: $5
   - Mini BBQ Chicken Pizza: $9
   - Mini Hawaiian Pizza: $10

   Expanded Budget Sheet
   - Cheese: $5 per pound
   - Pepperoni: $6 per pound
   - Veggies: $3 per pound
   - Chicken: $4 per pound
   - Pineapple: $2 per pound
   - BBQ Sauce: $3 per bottle

2. Problem Solving: "Pick 5 questions to solve with your business partner!"

   1. Cheese Pizza Sales
      - If the total sales for cheese pizzas are $720, how many cheese pizzas were sold?
   2. Pepperoni Pizza Ingredients
      - If you spent $483 on pepperoni, how many pounds of pepperoni did you buy?
   3. Veggie Pizza Sales
      - If the total sales for veggie pizzas are $408, how many veggie pizzas were sold?
   4. Margherita Pizza Ingredients
      - You sold 30 margherita pizzas during lunchtime! How many pounds of veggies can you buy from the money you made?
   5. BBQ Chicken Pizza Sales
      - If the total sales for BBQ chicken pizzas are $297 and each pizza costs $9, how many BBQ chicken pizzas were sold?
   6. Hawaiian Pizza Ingredients
      - If you spent $180 on pineapple for the Hawaiian pizzas, how many pounds of pineapple did you buy?

7. Total Cheese Cost

   - If you spent $225 on cheese on Week 1 and $140 on Week 2, how many pounds of cheese did you buy across both weeks?

8. Mixed Pizza Sales

   - If you sold 10 cheese pizzas, 15 pepperoni pizzas, and 5 veggie pizzas, what are the total sales? How many pounds of cheese can you buy with the money you made? Is there any money left over?

9. Ingredient Budgeting

   - You have $320 for ingredients this week. Buy as many whole pounds of chicken as possible. Is the remaining money enough to buy any other ingredients?

10. Profit Calculation

   - If the total sales for the day are $500 and the total cost of ingredients is $200, what is the profit? If you divide the day's profits among 6 people, how much money would each person get?

3. "Hold a board meeting! Have business partners get together and discuss their findings to make sure they're on the right track!"

Guided Practice

1. Divide 225 by 9 using the partial quotient method. Note: In all problems, students may use larger groups of the divisor (e.g., 20 or more groups) as they become more comfortable.

   Step 1: Estimate how many groups of 9 can be subtracted from 225. Start with 10 groups of 9 (which is 90). Subtract 90 from 225 to get 135.
   Step 2: Subtract another 90 from 135, leaving 45. That's another 10 groups.
   Step 3: Subtract 45 from 45, which leaves 0. That's 5 more groups.
   Step 4: Add the partial quotients: 10 + 10 + 5 = 25.

2. Divide 324 by 9 using the partial quotient method.

   Step 1: Estimate how many groups of 9 can be subtracted from 324. Start with 10 groups of 9 (which is 90). Subtract 90 from 324 to get 234.
   Step 2: Subtract another 90 from 234, leaving 144. That's another 10 groups.
   Step 3: Subtract another 90 from 144, leaving 54. That's another 10 groups.
   Step 4: Subtract 54 from 54, which leaves 0. That's 6 more groups.
   Step 5: Add the partial quotients: 10 + 10 + 10 + 6 = 36.

3. Divide 468 by 6 using the partial quotient method.

   Step 1: Estimate how many groups of 6 can be subtracted from 468. Start with 10 groups of 6 (which is 60). Subtract 60 from 468 to get 408.
   Step 2: Subtract another 60 from 408, leaving 348. That's another 10 groups.
   Step 3: Subtract another 60 from 348, leaving 288. That's another 10 groups.
   Step 4: Continue subtracting 60 until you reach 48. That's 7 groups of 10.
   Step 5: Subtract 48 from 48, which leaves 0. That's 8 more groups.
   Step 6: Add the partial quotients: 10 + 10 + 10 + 10 + 10 + 10 + 8 = 78.
   Step 7: The final quotient is 78.

Practice Questions

Name/Date _____

Fill in the Blanks

1. When using the partial quotient method, you subtract groups of the _____ from the _____.

2. $9 \times 10 =$ _____, and $9 \times 20 =$ _____.

3. If there is nothing left to divide after subtracting all the groups, the remainder is _____.

Multiple Choice

1. What is 156 divided by 12?

   A. 11

   B. 12

   C. 13

   D. 14

2. What is 468 divided by 6?

   A. 74

   B. 78

   C. 80

   D. 72

3. Which of the following is a correct partial quotient for 324 divided by 9?

   A. $9 \times 50 = 450$

   B. $9 \times 20 = 180$

   C. $90 \times 15 = 1,200$

   D. $10 \times 25 = 250$

Short Answer

1. How can the area model show the same information as the partial quotient method?

   _____

   _____

   _____

2. Samantha found 384 seashells on the beach. She wants to split them evenly into 8 jars. How many shells will go in each jar?

   _____

   _____

   _____

3. A baker has 252 cookies and wants to place them into boxes of 9. How many boxes will he need?

   _____

   _____

   _____

Open Response

Choose your own three-digit dividend and one-digit divisor. Solve using both the partial quotient method and the area model. Show all your work and explain which strategy you preferred and why. (Use the space on the bottom of the page to draw your area model.)

_____

_____

_____

_____

_____

Exit Ticket

1. Divide 189 by 9 using the partial quotient method. Show each step.

_____

_____

_____

2. How does the partial quotient method help you understand how many groups are in a number?

_____

_____

_____

Unit 2

OPERATIONS AND ALGEBRAIC THINKING

03 Understanding and Solving Problems

Notes from the Classroom

After 20 years of homeschooling my own 5 children, I returned to a public school classroom at the age of 53. Within one week I was asked the following questions by my 4th grade students: "Why do you have grandma hands?" "Do you think you will have any more babies?" and "Was Helen Keller one of your friends?"

–Lisa Orr
Melrose grade 4

Section 1: Writing Equations and Expressions

Have you ever compared how tall you are to how tall a friend is, or how many toys you have to how many your sibling has? These everyday comparisons become even more powerful when you use multiplication to measure them! Multiplicative comparison helps you ask questions like, "How many times taller am I than my little brother?" or "How many times more crayons does my friend have than me?" In this chapter, you'll transform these comparison stories into multiplication equations. By using visual models, drawings, and logic, you'll be able to solve real-world problems with confidence.

Learning Goals

I can (students will) represent and solve multiplicative comparison problems using multiplication equations, bar models, and number sense.

Teacher Tip

Begin teaching multiplicative comparison with concrete, real-world examples rather than abstract numbers. Ask questions like, "If Maya has three times as many pencils as Leo, and Leo has four pencils, how can we visually represent this?" Encourage students to use bar diagrams, repeated addition models, or number lines to illustrate their thinking. Clearly connecting concrete examples with equations (using a letter or symbol for unknown numbers) helps students solidify their understanding of this concept.

Lesson: Writing Equations and Expressions

Duration: 15–20 minutes

Intro

This set of standards includes 3 different skills: interpreting multiplication equations as a comparison, solving problems using multiplicative comparison, and determining whether an equation is true or false.

VIP Vocabulary

- Multiplicative Comparison: A comparison that expresses how much larger one quantity is than another by stating that the one is larger than the other "by a factor of ___" or that the one is a certain number of "times as large as" the other
- Equation: A mathematical statement that shows the equality between two expressions
- Unknown Number: A number that is not known and is represented by a symbol or letter in an equation
- Additive Comparison: A comparison that shows how much more one quantity is than another

---

Interpreting Multiplication Equations as a Comparison

This standard focuses on understanding multiplication as a comparison. It means interpreting a multiplication equation like $35 = 5 \times 7$ as a statement that 35 is 5 times as many as 7 and 7 times as many as 5. Students should be able to represent verbal statements of multiplicative comparisons as multiplication equations.

Looking for the Total (Missing Product)

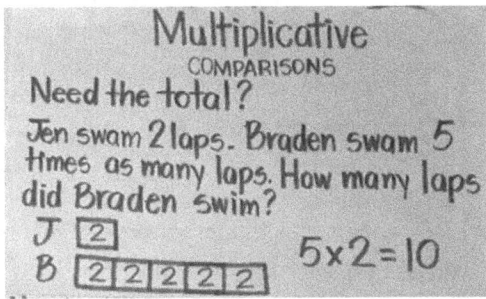

This kind of comparison gives you both parts (factors) but wants to know how much the larger amount has in total. You can use a tape diagram (also known as a strip diagram) to compare the two values and find the missing whole.

Here are some examples:

- A tree is 16 times as tall as a bush. If the bush is 2 feet tall, how tall is the tree? Total/Product : 16 × 2 = 32 feet
- Sarah has 4 times as many marbles as Tom. If Tom has 27 marbles, how many marbles does Sarah have? Total/Product : 4 × 27 = 108 marbles
- A recipe requires 5 times as much flour as sugar. If you use 12 cups of sugar, how much flour do you need? Total/Product : 5 × 12 = 60 cups of flour

To find the product, multiply the two factors together!

Let's Practice!

- Write: "A classroom has 3 times as many boys as girls. If there are 8 girls, how many boys are there?"
- Ask: "How should we label our two parts?" Answer: "Boys" and "girls." "Which part is larger?" Answer: Boys. There are 3 times as many of them.
- Draw: When we draw our model, the boys strip should be longer because there are more boys. There should be 3 times as many boy boxes than girl boxes.

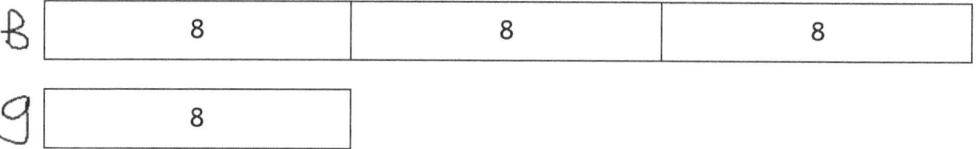

- Solve: 3 times more than 8 as an expression is 3 × 8.
- 3 × 8 = 24. There are 24 boys in the class.

Looking for the Smaller Part (Missing Factor)

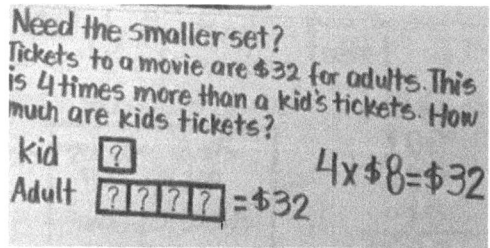

These comparisons give you the total (the product or largest number in the equation) and the larger part. They want you to solve for the smaller part of the comparison (this is not necessarily the smallest number in the equation). Using tape/strip diagrams and the inverse operation of division will help students solve with accuracy!

Here is an example:

- "A giraffe is 3 times as tall as a wolf. If the giraffe is 9 feet tall, how tall is the wolf?"
- Understand the problem. The giraffe is 3 times as tall as the wolf. Set up the diagram to visually see what you're solving for.

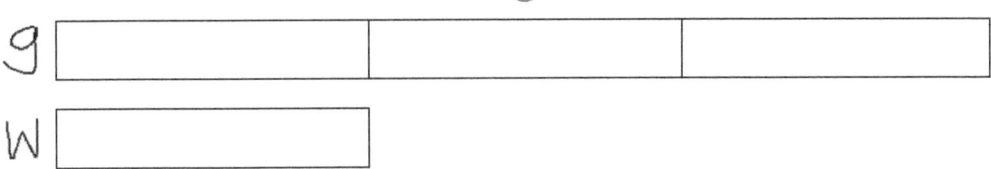

- Set up the equation: ___ × 3 = 9 OR 9 divided by 3 = __
- Solve the equation: 9 ÷ 3 = 3 and check your answer: 3 × 3 = 9 (Correct!)
- Write a solution statement so you know it makes sense! The wolf is 3 feet tall. The giraffe is 9 feet tall. The giraffe is 3 times as tall as the wolf.

Let's Practice!

- Write: "The mall is selling hats for $25 each. This is 5 times as much as a hat costs at Target. How much does a hat at Target cost?"
- Ask: "How should we label our two parts?" Answer: "Mall" and "Target." "Which part is larger?" Answer: The mall. A hat at the mall costs 5 times as much.
- Draw: "When we draw our model, the mall strip should be longer because the hats cost more at the mall. There should be 5 times as many mall boxes as Target boxes."
- Explain: "In this problem, we are labeling the whole of all the mall boxes, not individual boxes. All 5 of their boxes are equal to $25. If we know the total cost, how can we find the missing smaller part?"

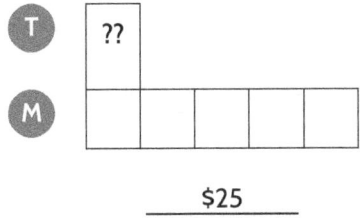

Looking for the Missing Comparison (Missing Factor)

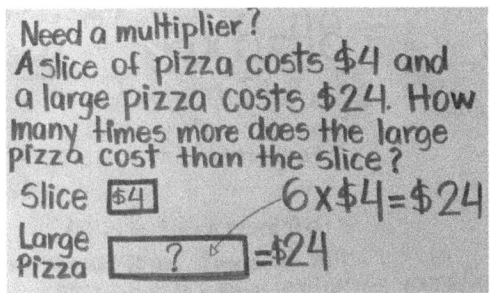

These comparisons give the total and one of the factors, but the comparative difference (the factor by which one quantity is larger than another) is unknown. When you draw the tape/strip diagrams, the number of boxes in the larger quantity is missing.

Here are some examples:

- "Brad and Anna go for a run over the weekend. Brad runs 3 miles. Anna runs 12 miles. Anna ran _____ times more miles than Brad."
- "If you use 20 cups of flour and 5 cups of sugar, how many times more flour do you need than sugar?"

Let's Practice!

"There were 48 kids at a birthday party. If there are 36 boys and 12 girls, how many times more boys are there than girls?"

- Understand the problem! A missing comparative difference (how many times more or less an amount is) is one of the factors in a multiplication problem. Use the inverse operation of multiplication (division!) to solve.
- Set up the equation: 36 is _____ times more than 12, so 36 = ____ × 12.
- Create a visual model to match. (Think: how many groups of 12 are in 36?)

Girls: 12	
Boys: 36	
How many groups of 12?	

Watch me teach it here:

PRO TIP It's easy for kids to mix up multiplicative comparison and additive comparison. Remember to look for the keyword "TIMES"! "More than" indicates the amount is increasing through addition, "times more" indicates the amount is increasing through multiplication!

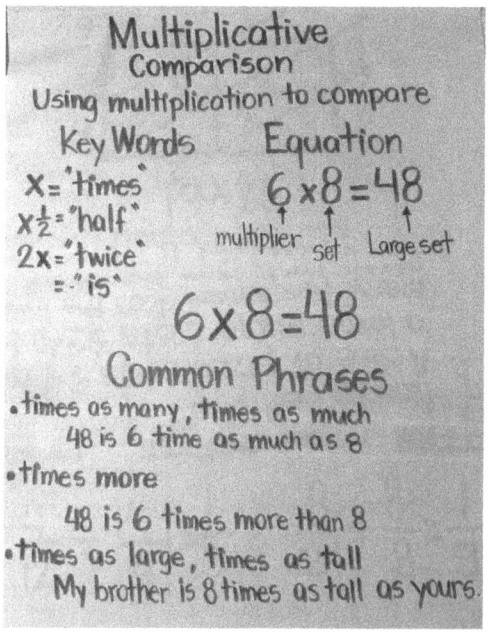

Connect It!

- Example 1: Comparing the length, weight, height, or age of 2 objects.
- Example 2: Comparing the distance between location A and location B with the distance between location A and location C either to determine how many times longer one distance is than the other or to determine by what fraction one distance is shorter than the other.
- Other examples: Comparing grades, prices, and salaries.

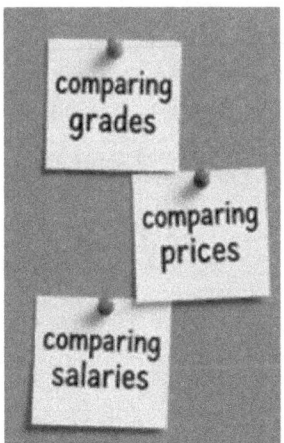

Team Talk: "Discuss places where you've seen multiplicative comparison in the real world." Have students share, and don't forget to add their responses to your anchor chart!

Hands-On Project: Visit a Farmers Market

Duration: 10–15 minutes

Materials

- Pencils
- Graphing paper

Intro

Your town has a farmers market each Saturday, and you are going to re-create it to show your class! Today, you will design the market stand by solving multiplicative comparison problems to determine the number of fruits, vegetables, and other items. Use the clues below to set up each stall and draw the number of items according to the clues!"

Activity Steps

1. Problem Solving

   - Clue 1: You have 3 times as many apples as oranges. If you have 4 oranges, how many apples do you have?
   - Clue 2: You have 5 times as many carrots as tomatoes. If you have 6 tomatoes, how many carrots do you have?
   - Clue 3: You have 2 times as many cucumbers as bell peppers. If you have 7 bell peppers, how many cucumbers do you have?
   - Clue 4: You have 4 times as many strawberries as blueberries. If you have 8 blueberries, how many strawberries do you have?
   - Clue 5: You have 3 times as many potatoes as onions. If you have 5 onions, how many potatoes do you have?
   - Clue 6: You have 6 times as many grapes as bananas. If you have 4 bananas, how many grapes do you have?
   - Clue 7: You have 2 times as many pumpkins as squash. If you have 9 squash, how many pumpkins do you have?
   - Clue 8: You have 5 times as many cherries as pears. If you have 3 pears, how many cherries do you have?
   - Clue 9: You have 4 times as many lettuce heads as cabbages. If you have 6 cabbages, how many lettuce heads do you have?
   - Clue 10: You have 3 times as many radishes as beets. If you have 7 beets, how many radishes do you have?

2. Gallery Walk

Have students post their completed markets on their desks or the wall, and let them take a gallery walk to check their classmates' thinking!

Guided Practice

1. Leo has 3 marbles. Maya has 4 times as many marbles as Leo. How many marbles does Maya have?

   Step 1: Identify known information: Leo has 3 marbles. Maya has 4 times as many.
   Step 2: Multiply to compare: 3 × 4 = 12.
   Step 3: Maya has 12 marbles.

2. A sunflower is 5 feet tall. A corn stalk is 3 times as tall as the sunflower. How tall is the corn stalk?

   Step 1: Identify the known information: sunflower = 5 feet, corn stalk is 3 times taller.
   Step 2: Multiply: 5 × 3 = 15.
   Step 3: The corn stalk is 15 feet tall.

3. Ava read 7 books. Her sister read 2 times as many books as Ava. How many books did her sister read?

   Step 1: Identify the known information: Ava read 7 books, her sister read 2 times more.
   Step 2: Multiply: 7 × 2 = 14.
   Step 3: Her sister read 14 books.

Practice Questions

Name/Date _____

Fill in the Blanks

1. Sarah has 5 pencils. Her friend has 3 times as many. Her friend has _____ pencils.

2. A book costs $9. A set of 4 books costs _____ dollars.

3. A flower is 2 inches tall. Another flower is 5 times as tall. It is _____ inches tall.

Multiple Choice

1. Noah has 6 toy cars. His cousin has 4 times as many. How many cars does Noah's cousin have?

   A. 10   C. 24

   B. 16   D. 36

2. A tree is 8 feet tall. A statue next to it is twice as tall. What is the height of the statue?

   A. 14 feet   C. 16 feet

   B. 10 feet   D. 18 feet

3. Liam earns $12 an hour. His older brother earns 3 times as much. How much does Liam's brother earn per hour?

   A. $24   C. $36

   B. $30   D. $48

Short Answer

1. Max has 7 apples. His brother has 4 times as many apples. How many apples does Max's brother have?

   _____

   _____

   _____

2. A movie ticket costs $8. How much do 6 tickets cost? Show your multiplication equation.

   _____

   _____

   _____

3. Emma has 9 stickers. Her collection is 3 times as big as her friend's. How many stickers does her friend have?

   _____

   _____

   _____

Open Response

Lena has 18 colored pencils, which is 3 times as many as her friend Jacob has. Write an equation that represents this situation. How many pencils does Jacob have? Explain clearly how you solved this problem using either multiplication or division.

_____

_____

_____

_____

_____

_____

Exit Ticket

1. A school has 5 times as many students as a nearby daycare. The daycare has 20 students. How many students does the school have?

   _____

   _____

   _____

2. A watermelon weighs 3 times as much as a cantaloupe. The cantaloupe weighs 4 pounds. How much does the watermelon weigh?

   _____

   _____

   _____

Notes from the Classroom

I was teaching third grade overseas in Malaysia. It was an American school, so instruction was in English. I had several Taiwanese students whose parents were in Malaysia for business. I was filling out forms for the Iowa test and had to ask each student for some information. I asked this little girl her birthdate. She answered a month and date. "What year?" I asked, all business. She hesitated, staring at me. I repeated, what year? Finally, she smiled, proud that she finally figured it out. "Every year!" (She wasn't wrong!)

–Nancy McMahan

Section 2: Multistep Word Problems

Fourth-grade students often feel overwhelmed by multistep word problems, especially when questions are presented in open-response formats. These types of problems require careful reading, planning, and problem-solving using more than one operation. In this lesson, students will learn how to break complex problems into manageable steps by slowing down, visualizing the scenario, and solving one operation at a time. To bring these ideas to life, we'll engage with the Numberock song "Multistep Word Problems," which models strategies for tackling multistep tasks in a fun, musical format.

Learning Goals

I can (students will) solve multistep word problems using all four operations (addition, subtraction, multiplication, and division) and determine whether answers make sense in the context of the problem.

Teacher Tip

Introducing acronyms like CUBES (Circle key numbers, Underline the question, Box important words, Evaluate what steps to take, Solve and check) provides a repeatable structure for students. These strategies help learners slow down, organize their thinking, and avoid skipping steps.

Whole Brain Teaching

Bring the chorus of the Numberock song to life with simple movements:

"Multistep problems might cause you fright" – Students raise hands and duck down as if scared.
"Just slow down and you'll see the light" – Slowly rise with arms lifted and point to their eyes, then upward.
"Solve one step at a time" – Take small, deliberate steps forward.
"The answer you seek, you will find!" – Reach hands outward and then pull inward toward the heart.

These movements help kinesthetic learners internalize the process of step-by-step problem solving.

Notes from the Classroom

During a unit on word problems, I started reading: "If a train leaves Chicago at 3 p.m.–"

Immediately, Noah raised his hand. "Why is it *always* Chicago?" Before I could answer, someone else said, "Who takes the train anymore?" Then, "Why do they always buy so much in these problems? Who gets **42** apples?"

We eventually figured out what time the trains met, and also established that most of the class prefers airplanes, New York and a smaller amount of fruit.

–Mrs. Hill

Lesson: Multistep Word Problems

Duration: 15–20 minutes

Intro

When you're solving multistep problems, critical thinking is a must! Students need to analyze word problems to determine the operations needed, create and solve equations that represent the problems, explain their reasoning, and interpret the solutions in the context of the problem.

VIP Vocabulary

- Multistep Problem: A math problem that requires more than one operation (addition, subtraction, multiplication, or division) to solve
- Operation: A mathematical process such as addition (+), subtraction (−), multiplication (×), or division (÷)
- Remainder: The amount left over after division when one number does not divide the other number exactly
- Estimate: To find an approximate value that is close to the exact answer

Let's Rock!

Now's a great time to play Numberock's "Multistep Word Problems" song!

Multistep Word Problems	
https://numberock.com/mttm/	

CUBES

"We can use the acronym CUBES to help us break multistep problems into more manageable chunks!"

Write: Sarah has 45 apples. She wants to put them into baskets. Each basket can hold 6 apples. How many baskets does she need, and how many apples will be left over?

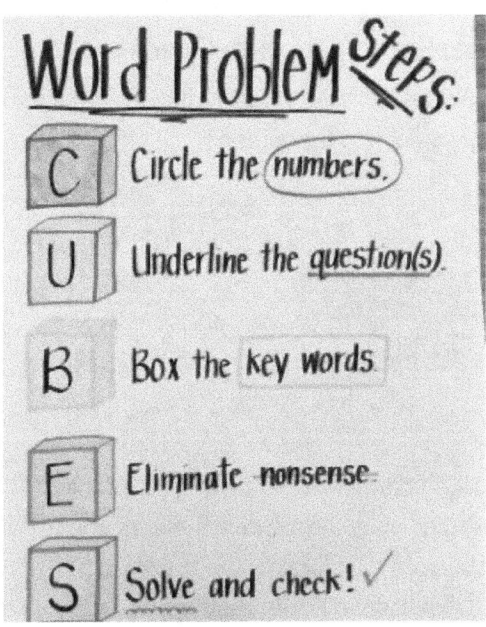

Have students help identify all the parts of the problem, following the steps of CUBES.

Step 1: "Circle the important numbers and labels in the problem (45 apples and 6 apples)."

Step 2: "Underline the question(s): 'How many baskets does she need, and how many apples will be left over?'"

Step 3: "Box the key words ('each basket can hold,' 'will be left over')."

Step 4: "Eliminate and Evaluate: Get rid of any distractors. Ask questions about what is happening in the story. (Sarah is SPLITTING her apples into equal groups, so we will be dividing. What is LEFT OVER is going to be the remainder.)"

Step 5: "Solve and Check: Divide the total number of apples by the number of apples each basket can hold. $45 \div 6 = 7$ R3. Sarah will need 7 baskets (using 42 apples), and there will be 3 apples left over."

Solution Statement: "Sarah needs 7 baskets, and she will have 3 apples left over."

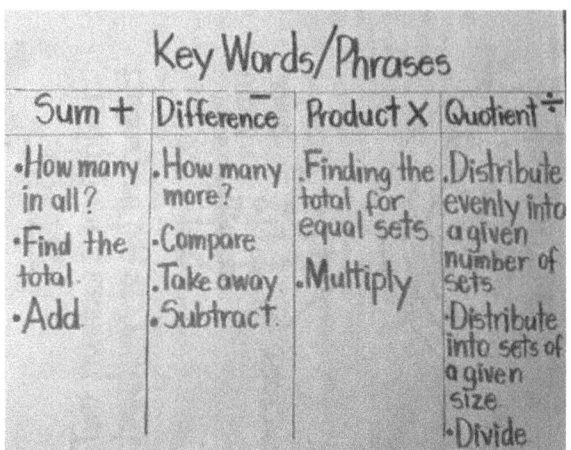

Watch me teach it here:

PRO TIP Encourage students to put themselves into the word problem and imagine they are the ones completing the steps! Drawing or acting out the problem with a partner can also be very beneficial in understanding what the problem is asking!

Understand, Choose, Solve, Double-Check

Write: A gardener plants 8 rows of flowers with 12 flowers in each row. Later, he removes 15 flowers. How many flowers are left in the garden?

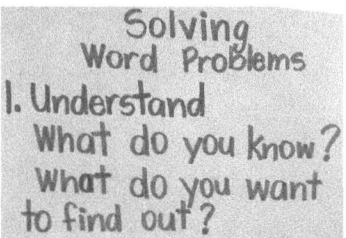

Here's a guide to walk students through solving the problem in manageable pieces!

Understand: Understand that the gardener **plants** some flowers **in rows** and then **removes** some flowers. Visualize the planting and the removal.

Choose a Strategy: Use charts, models, estimate and use patterns!

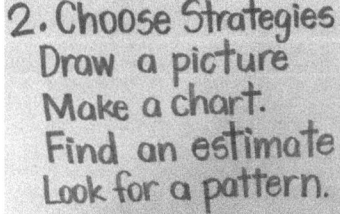

Use keywords to help decide on which operations to use: Multiplication ("in each row") and subtraction ("removes").

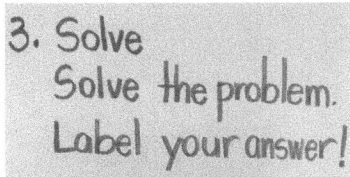

Break Down the Problem: **Multiply** to find how many total flowers are planted (8 rows of 12). **Subtract** to find out how many flowers are left after the gardener removes 15.

Solve:

$8 \times 12 = 96$

$96 - 15 = 81$

Solution Statement: There are 81 flowers left in the garden.

Double-Check: Estimate to check that your answer is reasonable!

Connect It!

Example 1: Planning a party

Example 2: Taking a road trip

Other examples: Fundraising, gardening, shopping for clothes

Team Talk: "Discuss places where you've had to solve multistep problems in the real world." Have students share, and don't forget to add their responses to your anchor chart!

Hands-On Project: Problem/Solution Match

Duration: 5–10 minutes

Materials

- Pencils
- Index cards (1 per student)
- Paper

Intro

"Today we are going to apply our understanding of how to solve 2-step problems by creating our own. On the front of the index card, create a word problem with multiple steps (using 2 different operations). On the back of the card, write the equation and steps used to solve your problem."

Activity Steps

Problem Solving

1. Give students 10–15 minutes to partner with their classmates and solve each other's problems on their paper. When partners are finished solving, have students flip their cards over to the solution and compare answers. If both partners agree, switch partners and continue until the timer has gone off.

2. Record problems and solutions on anchor charts and post around the room to use as a reference tool throughout the unit.

Guided Practice

1. Lexi has 3 baskets. Each basket holds 4 apples. She buys 6 more apples. How many apples does she have now?

   Step 1: $3 \times 4 = 12$
   Step 2: $12 + 6 = 18$
   Final Answer: 18 apples

2. Carlos read 45 pages on Monday and 38 pages on Tuesday. He wants to read 100 pages this week. How many more pages must he read?

   Step 1: $45 + 38 = 83$
   Step 2: $100 - 83 = 17$
   Final Answer: 17 pages

3. A camping trip started with 60 granola bars. If 3 campers each ate 4 bars, and 5 bars were given away, how many bars are left?

   Step 1: $3 \times 4 = 12$
   Step 2: $12 + 5 = 17$
   Step 3: $60 - 17 = 43$ granola bars

Practice Questions

Name/Date _____

Fill in the Blanks

1. When solving a multistep problem, we should always make a _____.

2. In the expression $(49 - 4) \div 5$, we must subtract before we _____.

3. A _____ problem requires more than one operation to solve.

Multiple Choice

1. During a basketball game, Big Paul made 8 shots worth 2 points and 5 shots worth 3 points. How many total points did he score?

   A. 26
   B. 31
   C. 34
   D. 35

2. Mia has 4 shelves. Each shelf holds 6 books, and these shelves are all full. She buys 10 more books. How many books will she have?

   A. 44
   B. 34
   C. 24
   D. 40

3. Which problem matches this equation: $(49 - 4) \div 5$?

   A. 49 logs were split into 4 piles, and 5 logs were burned.

   B. 45 logs were split into 4 piles.

   C. Out of a total of 49 logs, 4 were burned and the rest divided equally into 5 piles.

   D. 5 logs were burned, and 49 were left.

Short Answer

1. A student biked 44 miles the first day and 80 miles the second day. She wanted to bike 200 miles total. How many more miles does she need to ride?

_____

_____

_____

2. Carmen baked 36 cookies and gave 12 to her neighbors. Then she split the rest evenly among 3 friends. How many cookies did each friend get?

_____

_____

_____

3. Derek bought 5 packs of markers with 4 in each pack. He gave away 6 markers to friends. How many markers does he have left?

_____

_____

_____

Open Response

Create a multistep word problem that uses at least two operations. Then, solve it and explain how you figured out each step.

_____

_____

_____

_____

_____

Exit Ticket

1. A hiker walks 12 miles on Monday and 15 miles on Tuesday, and wants to walk 40 miles in total. How many more miles does the hiker need to walk?

_____

_____

_____

2. Elias collects toy cars. He buys 3 packs with 6 cars in each, then gives 4 cars to his cousin. How many cars does Elias have left?

_____

_____

_____

Notes from the Classroom

During our rounding unit this year, the goal was simple: round numbers to the nearest ten. The reality was . . . well, less simple.

I started strong. I had the chart, the anchor poster, even the catchy rhyme:

"Five or more, raise the score! Four or less, let it rest!"

Everybody was in sync.

Then I wrote 47 on the board and asked, "Ok guys, what do we round 47 to?"

"Forty!" several kids shouted. A few yelled "fifty!" and one student, who I suspect just likes to cause chaos, yelled "three hundred!"

"Okay," I said, "let's use the rhyme."

They dutifully recited it again – *five or more, raise the score!* – and then someone raised their hand and asked, "What if it's **44.9**?"

We had not discussed decimals. We were not *supposed* to be rounding decimals.

"Then it's still forty," I said, praying no one else noticed the rabbit hole opening beneath us.

But of course, another hand shot up. "What if it's **44.99999**?"

Hilarious. Suddenly everyone wants to debate.

Then, from the back, a kid named Tyler – who had been staring at the ceiling for most of the lesson – looked down at his paper and said, "I just don't think numbers should change who they are just because of where they're standing."

I paused. "That's. . . fair," I said.

He nodded solemnly. "Forty-seven wants to be forty-seven. We shouldn't make it fifty just because we feel like it."

So I guess rounding has now become an existential issue.

I can't wait to find out who thinks the numerator has feelings.

–B. Morris

Section 3: Factors and Multiples

Strong multiplication fluency opens the door to richer ideas such as factors, multiples, prime, composite, and square numbers. These terms help students classify numbers and prepare for fraction work and algebra later on. A factor is a number that divides another number evenly. A multiple is the product of a number and a counting number. A prime number has exactly two factors (1 and itself), while a composite number has more than two. Finally, a square number is a special case: a number that is the product of a whole number times itself. Numberock's song "Prime, Composite, & Square" turns this vocabulary into an unforgettable tune, embedding definitions into students' memories through rhythm and rhyme.

Learning Goals

I can (students will) list factors of any whole number ≤ 100, generate multiples of one-digit numbers, and determine whether a number is prime, composite, or square.

Teacher Tip

Students often mix up factors and multiples. Anchor factors to division (numbers that "fit inside") and multiples to multiplication (skip-counting products). Use a factor T-chart for 24 (1 × 24, 2 × 12, 3 × 8, 4 × 6) and a multiples list for 6 (6, 12, 18, 24 . . .). Linking the vocabulary to known operations reinforces meaning.

Whole Brain Learning

To make the concepts of square, prime, and composite numbers engaging and memorable, use dance movements to reinforce the definitions and properties of each number type, encouraging whole-brain learning through physical activity and repetition:

Square numbers: Students form a square with bent arms and step in a box pattern.
Prime numbers: Hold up one finger on one hand and a fist in the other.
Composite numbers: Clap three times to represent that they have 3 or more factors.
These moves engage visual, auditory, and kinesthetic learners while the song plays.

Lesson: Factors and Multiples

Duration: 15–20 minutes

Intro

Understanding factors and multiples can help in real-life situations, such as dividing items into equal groups or understanding patterns in numbers, but it can be tricky to remember which one is which!

VIP Vocabulary

- Factor: A number that divides another number without leaving a remainder
- Multiple: The product of a number and any whole number
- Prime Number: A number greater than 1 that has no factors other than 1 and itself
- Composite Number: A number greater than 1 that has more than two factors

---

- Do: Write down the number 12 on the board.
- Say: "Let's think about the number 12 in two different ways. **Multiples** are like the results you get when you keep adding the same number over and over (skip-counting). Imagine you have a jump rope and you jump 12 times each round. If you keep jumping, you get
  - 12 jumps in the first round
  - 24 jumps in the second round (12 + 12)
  - 36 jumps in the third round (12 + 12 +12)

  So, the numbers 12, 24, 36 and so on are MULTIPLES of 12 because they are the results of multiplying 12 by whole numbers (1, 2, 3, etc.)."
- Ask: "How many multiples can a number have?" The number of multiples is infinite. "Are multiples larger or smaller than the original number?" Larger.
- Say: "Now let's think about 12 as our total. **Factors** are like the building blocks of a number. Imagine you have a set of LEGO bricks. If you want to build a tower that is exactly 12 bricks tall, you can use different combinations of bricks to make it. For example: You can use 3 bricks and stack them 4 times ($3 \times 4 = 12$). You can use 2 bricks and stack them 6 times ($2 \times 6 = 12$), or you can stack 1 brick at a time and stack them 12 times ($1 \times 12 = 12$). So, the numbers 1, 2, 3, 4, 6, and 12 are factors of 12 because they can be multiplied together to make 12."
- Ask: "How can I find a different way to make 12 by creating equal groups?" Dividing. "Are the amounts in the group bigger or smaller than 12?" Smaller.
- Say: "Today we're going to find MULTIPLES and FACTORS of different numbers and decide what operation to use to solve."

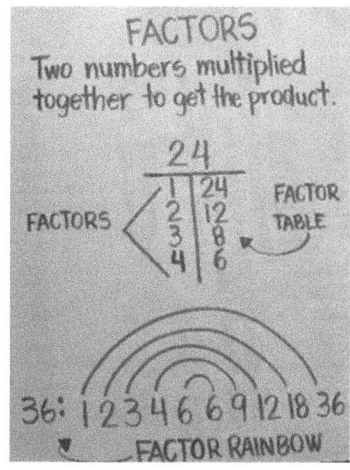

PRO TIP A great way to remember the difference between factors and multiples is to use some easy-to-learn dance moves! "We MULTIPLY multiples, they go higher! We BREAK DOWN the factors, they go lower!"

Watch me teach it here:

Multiples

A multiple of a number is the product of that number and any whole number.

ex. Find the first 5 multiples of:

3: 3,6,9,12,15...
9: 9,18,27,36,45...
10: 10,20,30,40,50...

they go on indefinitely!

Let's Rock!

Now's a great time to play Numberock's "Prime, Composite, Square" song!

Prime, Composite, Square
https://numberock.com/mttm/

Questions Before, During, and After the Song

Before: "Have you ever heard of "prime" or "composite" numbers? What do you think they might mean?"

During: "Pause at 1:19. At least how many arrays can you make with a composite number? When they showed a *prime number*, what made it different from the composite numbers?"

"What visual or rhyme helped you remember what composite numbers are?"

After: "Can you name two numbers that have some of the same factors? What about the same multiples? Which number from the video was *prime*? How do you know it's prime?"

How could you use what you learned to solve a problem like:

"I have 12 apples and want to share them evenly among friends—how many ways can I do that?"

What was one song lyric or visual that helped you remember the idea of factors or multiples?

Factors

Intro

There are a few different ways to find all the factor pairs of a number, but the most important part is having a system to make sure you don't miss any!

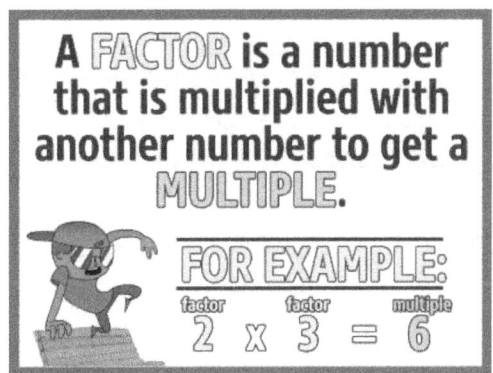

- Table: A table can keep factors organized by listing the digits 1-10 on the left side and identifying any possible matches on the right side. This helps students go in numerical order and not skip any factors.

- Factor Rainbow: (my favorite!) Factor Rainbows are helpful in name alone! Students can visually see the larger number being broken down into smaller parts and which numbers are part of the same factor pair. More than one arch on the rainbow means the number is composite, only one arch means it is prime!

- Partner Practice: "You want to plant a garden with 18 flowers. What are all the different ways you can plant your garden in rows and columns? Find all the factor pairs!"

Multiples

Intro

Finding multiples is as easy as skip-counting! Reminding students that they have already learned their multiples when they first learned to multiply can put them at ease.

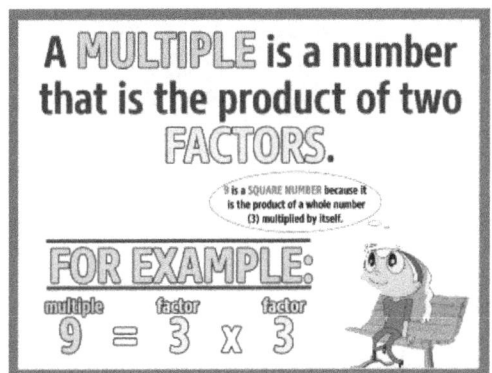

- Ask: "If you want to know how many pizzas you need for a big party, you can use multiples. If each pizza has 8 slices and you need 40 slices, how many pizzas should you order?" You may want to follow up with a further question: "How many groups of 8 are in 40?"

Partner Practice: If each pizza had 5 pieces, how many total pieces could there be if they ordered up to 6 pizzas? You may want to follow up with a hint: "Find the first 6 multiples of 5."

Connect It!

"Factors and multiples are everywhere! Where do you see them?"

Multiples

- Example 1 – Scheduling Events: If a conference is held every 3 months, the months when the conference occurs are multiples of 3 (e.g., March, June, September, December).
- Example 2 – Packaging: If a box can hold 12 items, then the total number of items in multiple boxes will be multiples of 12 (e.g., 12, 24, 36).
- More examples of multiples: financial planning, budgeting, making multiple batches of recipes.

Factors

- Example 1 – Dividing Resources: If you have 30 apples and want to divide them equally among friends, the number of friends must be a factor of 30.
- Example 2 – Construction: When you're building a rectangular garden, the dimensions (length and width) must be factors of the total area. For example, if the area is 24 square meters, possible dimensions could be 2×12, 3×8, or 4×6 meters.
- Other examples: Cooking, arranging desks in a classroom, dividing something equally among friends, music beats, game scoring.

Team Talk: "Discuss places where you've seen factors and multiples." Have students share, and don't forget to add their responses to your anchor chart!

Hands-On Activity: Planning a Baking Day

Duration: 10–15 minutes

Materials

- Paper, pencils, and colored markers (optional)

Intro

"Today you are going to help plan a baking day. In order to bake the cookies, muffins, and cupcakes, you need to provide the specific ingredients the recipe requires. You'll need to determine the total quantities based on the number of batches you want to make."

Activity Steps

1. Provide the students with the basic recipes:

   - Cookies: 2 cups of flour, 1 cup of sugar, 1 cup of butter (makes 12 cookies)
   - Muffins: 3 cups of flour, 2 cups of sugar, 1 cup of butter (makes 8 muffins)
   - Cupcakes: 2 cups of flour, 2 cups of sugar, 1 cup of butter (makes 6 cupcakes)

      Ask students to decide how many of each item they want to make. For example, 36 cookies, 24 muffins, and 48 cupcakes. Students will find the FACTORS of each amount before moving to the next step.
   - Cookies: Factors of 36 (1, 2, 3, 4, 6, 9, 12, 18, 36)
   - Muffins: Factors of 24 (1, 2, 3, 4, 6, 8, 12, 24)
   - Cupcakes: Factors of 48 (1, 2, 3, 4, 6, 8, 12, 16, 24, 48)

2. Using the factor list, have students determine how many batches of each item they are making.

   - Cookies: To make 36 cookies, find the factor that goes with 12. 12 × 3 = 36, so you will need to make 3 batches.
   - Muffins: To make 24 muffins, find the factor that goes with 8. 8 × 3 = 24, so you will need to make 3 batches.
   - Cupcakes: To make 48 cupcakes, find the factor that goes with 6. 6 × 8 = 48, so you will need to make 8 batches.

3. Calculate the total quantity of each ingredient needed for all the items:

   - Cookies: 3 batches × (2 cups of flour, 1 cup of sugar, 1 cup of butter)
   - Muffins: 3 batches × (3 cups of flour, 2 cups of sugar, 1 cup of butter)
   - Cupcakes: 8 batches × (2 cups of flour, 2 cups of sugar, 1 cup of butter)

4. Have the students draw a shopping list with the total quantity of each ingredient.

Lesson: Patterns

Duration: 15–20 minutes

Intro

Students will create and explain their own numerical patterns using a rule, and identify how the pattern changes.

VIP Vocabulary

- Pattern: A repeated or predictable sequence of numbers or shapes
- Rule: The operation used to create the pattern (e.g., add 3, multiply by 2)
- Sequence: An ordered list of numbers that follow a rule

- Ask: "What's a pattern you've seen in math or nature?" (skip counting, doubling, multiplication tables, multiples)

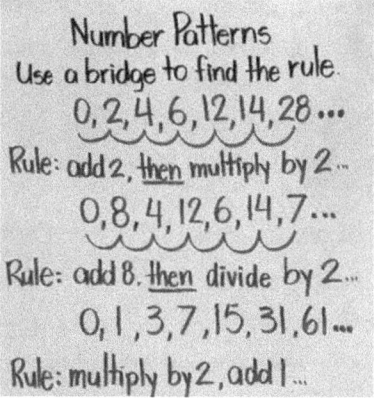

- Say: "Patterns are everywhere in math! They can be shape patterns or numerical patterns. The goal is to find the RULE so you can continue the SEQUENCE! Using a bridge can be really helpful."
- Do: Write this pattern on the board: 0, 2, 4, 6, 12, 14, 28...
- Ask: "Is this pattern increasing or decreasing? What operations can we consider if it's increasing? (addition and multiplication) What operations can we consider if it's decreasing? (subtraction and division)."
- Say: "Some patterns follow 2 step rules. In this example, we add 2, then multiply 2 and continue the sequence by following the rules. The bridge lets us see how the pattern changes and then repeats."

Guided Practice

1. List all factors of 18.

   1, 2, 3, 6, 9, 18. So it's composite.

2. Write the first five multiples of 7.

   7, 14, 21, 28, 35.

3. Is 36 prime, composite, or square? Prove it.

   Square (6 × 6) and composite. Its factors are 1, 2, 3, 4, 6, 9, 12, 18, and 36.

Practice Questions

Name/Date _____

Fill in the Blanks

1. A number that has exactly two factors is called _____.

2. Multiples of 8 end in 0, 8, 6, 4, or _____.

3. The first square number greater than 16 is _____.

Multiple Choice

1. Which number is prime?

   A. 21   **C.** 23

   B. 25   **D.** 27

2. The factor pairs of 30 are 1 × 30, 2 × 15, 3 × 10, and 5 × 6. 30 is

   A. Prime   **C.** Square

   B. Composite   **D.** None of the above

3. 49 is a square because it's the product of

   A. 7 × 6   **C.** 7 × 7

   B. 5 × 10   **D.** 4 × 12

Short Answer

1. Give two composite numbers between 10 and 20 and list a factor pair for each.

   _____

   _____

   _____

2. Explain why 1 is neither prime nor composite.

   _____

   _____

   _____

3. Create a square array to show that 25 is a square number. How many rows and columns does the array have?

Open Response

Design a "number poster" for any number between 10 and 50. Your poster must include the following:

- all factor pairs (make drawings of the arrays)
- the first four multiples of the number
- a statement classifying it as prime, composite, square, or more than one
- two sentences explaining real-world uses (e.g., arrays in gardens, rows of seats)

Exit Ticket

1. From the following list of numbers, record all that are factors of 32: 2, 4, 5, 6, 8, 16.

_____

_____

_____

2. What is the 6th multiple of 9?

_____

_____

_____

Fraction Concepts

Section 1: Equivalent Fractions

Imagine you and a friend each have half a pizza, but your half is cut into two slices, and your friend's half is just one big slice. Who has more pizza? If you said neither, you're thinking like a mathematician! Both of you have equivalent fractions, which we can define as "fractions that look different but have the same value." Fourth graders get to dive deep into this fascinating world, exploring how fractions like 1/2, 2/4, and 4/8 can all represent the same amount. With Numberock's energetic Latin-inspired tune "Equivalent Fractions," you'll discover through music and rhythm why fractions like 3/9 and 1/3 share equal space on a number line, and you'll remember that "equivalent fractions is the name . . . for fractions whose values are the same!"

Learning Goals

I can (students will) recognize, generate, and explain equivalent fractions using visual models, multiplication, and division.

Teacher Tip

Kick off the lesson with a scenario your students will love . . . pizza! Ask them to imagine a pizza cut into four slices. If you take one slice (1/4 of the pizza) and then cut your slice into two smaller slices, you now have 2/8. Did the amount you have actually change? Students will immediately see that they still have the same amount of pizza, but that it's just cut differently. Transition from this intuitive and conceptual understanding of equivalent fractions to fraction bars and number lines. This approach helps students visually grasp the idea of equivalence before moving on to more abstract multiplication and division methods.

Whole Brain Teaching

Bring the lesson to life with Numberock's "Equivalent Fractions" song. Guide your students through coordinated movements as they listen to the bridge rap: when they hear "multiply the top and bottom by the same number," they clap upward for "top" and downward for "bottom." On the phrase "on top and under," students alternate pointing up and down rhythmically. For the words "numerator, denominator," they fist pump upward on "numerator" and then downward on "denominator." These rhythmic and kinesthetic activities will help students internalize key concepts and vocabulary, creating lasting mathematical memories.

Lesson: Equivalent Fractions

Duration: 15-20 minutes

Intro

There are a few ways to find equivalent fractions, depending on the student's level of understanding on the foundation of fractions and their overall number sense. A great place to start is with models and numbers lines, and then you can move to multiplication/division as students get more comfortable! The butterfly method is a great way to self-correct!

VIP Vocabulary

- Fraction: A way to represent a part of a whole
- Numerator: The top number in a fraction, the one that shows how many parts we have
- Denominator: The bottom number in a fraction, the one that shows how many equal parts the whole is divided into
- Equivalent Fractions: Different fractions that represent the same part of a whole

---

Models and Number Lines

If fraction bars and circle manipulatives are available, they're a great support for students in the concrete stage of learning.

- Do: Draw a pizza on the board and divide it into 4 equal parts. Shade in 2 of the parts.
- Ask: "If I eat 2 out of these 4 slices (the shaded part of our model), what fraction of the pizza have I eaten?"
- Say: "That's right! I ate 2/4 of the pizza. But my best friend said I actually ate 1/2 of the pizza. Are they right? Am I wrong?" Have students discuss and share out their thinking.
- Ask: "How can a model help prove or disprove our thinking?"

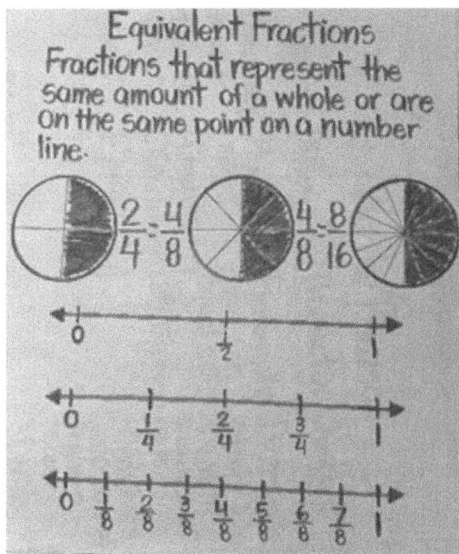

Watch me teach it here:

PRO TIP Accuracy is key when we're using models and number lines! Remind students that the wholes need to be the exact same size and that they need to be careful when dividing their models to make sure they can really see the equivalency!

Let's Rock!

Now's a great time to play Numberock's "Equivalent Fractions" song!

Equivalent Fractions Song

Equivalent Fractions	
https://numberock.com/mttm/	

Questions Before, During, and After the Song

Before: "Can two fractions look different but still represent the same amount? Give an example you already know."

During: Pause at 0:30: "How does Numberock use socks to show that 1/2 is equivalent to 2/4? Explain the visual example."

After: "How could you use multiplication to find an equivalent fraction for 1/3? Explain your method and show your result."

Let's Practice!

- Say: "We figured out that 2/4 and 1/2 are EQUIVALENT fractions because they represent the same part of the whole. Let's use models and number lines to identify other fractions that are equal to 1/2."
- ENRICH: "What do you notice about the equivalent fractions? How could we find additional fractions that are equivalent to 1/2 WITHOUT using a model or number line?"

    Partner Practice: "Finn says that 3/4 and 2/3 are equivalent fractions. Is he correct? How can you prove your answer?"

Multiplication and Division to Find Equivalent Fractions

Intro

We can multiply or divide a fraction by another fraction that is equal to 1 to create EQUIVALENT fractions.

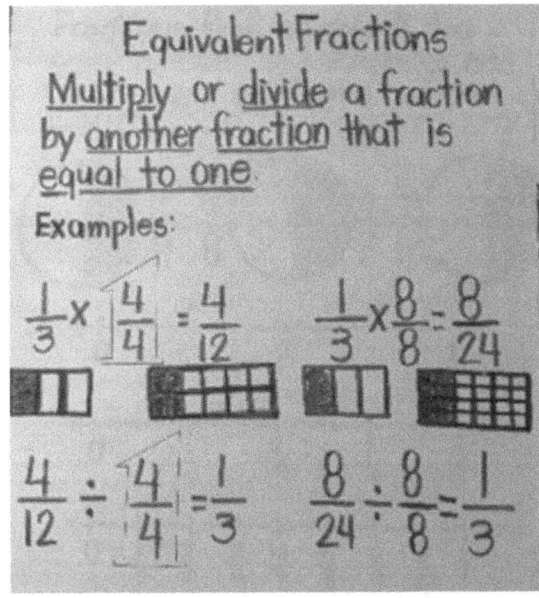

- Do: Write the following fractions on the board: 2/2, 4/4, 10/10, 1/1.
- Ask: "What do all of these fractions have in common?" They are all equal to 1 whole. "What happens to a number when we multiply or divide it by 1?" The number stays the same; this is the IDENTITY PROPERTY of multiplication and division.
- Do: Write $1/3 \times 2/2$ on the board. Ask students to predict what will happen to the product. Answer: It will be equal to 1/3. Repeat by multiplying 1/3 by other fractions equal to 1 whole.
- Ask: "What do you notice about all of the fractions we've created?" and "What do you think will happen if we divide fractions by fractions equivalent to 1 whole?"
- Do: Use examples from the multiplication problem above to demonstrate this idea in reverse!

Let's Practice!

- Say: "Imagine we have a cookie cake cut into 16 pieces and your family eats 8 of the pieces. The next week, you buy another cookie cake and it's cut into only 8 pieces. How many pieces would need to be eaten to equal the amount your family ate the week before?"

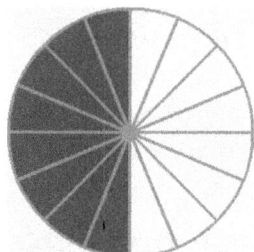

- Ask: "What do we need to divide 16 by to get 8? What happens when we also divide the numerator (8) by the amount?" "Can we divide the numerator and denominator by another fraction equal to 1?" Yes! You can divide it by 4/4 to get 2/4 or divide it by 8/8 to get 1/2. "What else can we do (besides divide) to 8/16 to get another equivalent fraction?" Multiply by fractions equal to 1.

Butterfly Method (Cross Multiplication)

Students can use cross multiplication (otherwise known as the butterfly method) to self-check their thinking, but it's preferably not used as a first method of instruction because it doesn't explain the WHY behind equivalent fractions. It is, however, used well in conjunction with the other strategies described above. Simply multiply the digits across from each other in the butterfly wings. If both products are equal, so are the fractions!

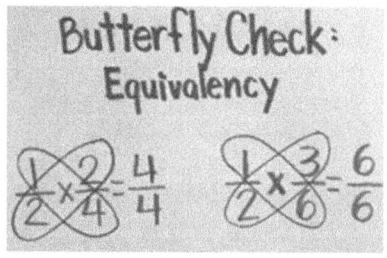

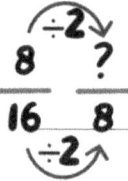

Connect It!

"Equivalent fractions are everywhere – where do you spy some?"

- Example 1 – Baking and Cooking: Explain how equivalent fractions are used in cooking. If a recipe calls for 1/2 cup of sugar, but you only have a 1/4 cup measuring cup, you can use two 1/4 cups to make 1/2 cup because 1/2 is equivalent to 2/4.

- Example 2 – Time Management: If you spend 30 minutes reading a book, you've spent 30/60 of an hour reading. This is the same as 1/2 hour because 30/60 is equivalent to 1/2.
- Other examples: Money, construction measurements, cutting up pizzas and other foods.

Team Talk: "Discuss places where you've seen equivalent fractions." Have students share, and don't forget to add their responses to your anchor chart!

Hands-On Activity: Fraction Match

Objective
Students will use fraction bars or other manipulatives to match equivalent fractions.

Materials

- Fraction bars or paper strips
- Pencils
- Colored markers (optional)

Prep

Place students in pairs or groups and pass out one bag of fractions bars or fraction circles per group.

Game Rules

- **Round 1: Matching Fractions (5 minutes)**
  Partner 1 creates a fraction using the fraction bars or circles. Partner 2 then tries to create equivalent fractions with a different set of fractions. "Line up the bars or circles to check for equivalence. Take turns creating the first fraction until the timer goes off."
- **Round 2: Match the Teacher (5 minutes)**
  The teacher writes a fraction on the board (e.g., 2/3). Students have 1 minute to create as many equivalent fractions as possible with their manipulatives. Discuss as a class and write equivalent fractions on the board to check with butterfly method.

Guided Practice

1. "Create equivalent fractions for 1/5 by multiplying numerator and denominator by 2 and then by 3.

   Step 1: $1/5 \times 2/2 = 2/10$
   Step 2: $1/5 \times 3/3 = 3/15$
   Equivalent fractions: 2/10 and 3/15."

2. "Simplify 6/18 by dividing numerator and denominator by 6.

   Step 1: $6 \div 6 = 1$
   Step 2: $18 \div 6 = 3$
   Equivalent fraction: 1/3."

3. "Use a number line to show that 2/6 is equivalent to 1/3. Draw both fractions on a number line from 0 to 1 and see they fall on the exact same spot."

Practice Questions

Name/Date _____

Fill in the Blanks

1. Fractions that represent the same value are called _____ fractions.
2. You can find equivalent fractions by multiplying or dividing both numerator and denominator by the _____ number.
3. On a number line, 1/2, 2/4, and 4/8 all represent the _____ value.

Multiple Choice

1. Which fraction is equivalent to 2/3?

   A. 4/5   C. 6/8

   B. 4/6   D. 8/10

2. Simplify the fraction 10/15. What is the simplified equivalent fraction?

   A. 1/2   C. 3/4

   B. 2/3   D. 4/5

3. Which pair of fractions shows equivalence on the number line?

   A. 2/5 and 4/9   C. 3/4 and 6/8

   B. 3/6 and 2/3   D. 5/7 and 3/4

Short Answer

1. Simplify 4/12 to its simplest equivalent fraction. Explain how you did this.

   _____

   _____

   _____

2. Name two equivalent fractions for 3/5. Show your work clearly.

_____

_____

_____

3. Why can't you find an equivalent fraction for 2/5 by dividing numerator and denominator by 3? Explain clearly.

_____

_____

_____

Open Response

Imagine your friend tells you that they ate 4/8 of a chocolate bar, and you say you ate half of yours. Did one of you eat more chocolate, or did you eat the same amount? Use fraction bars and a number line to clearly show and explain your answer.

Exit Ticket

1. Write two fractions equivalent to 3/4. Show clearly how you found them.

_____

_____

2. Why does multiplying the numerator and denominator by the same number produce an equivalent fraction? Explain in your own words.

_____

_____

Notes from the Classroom

During a lesson on comparing fractions. I asked my class, "Which is bigger: $\frac{1}{2}$ or $\frac{1}{3}$?"

Immediately a student raised his hand and said, "Depends who you ask."

I burst out laughing but he was so serious. "Okay. . .", I said, "I'm asking *you*."

He shrugged. "Half *feels* smaller, but the model looks bigger, so I don't trust it."

Honestly, that's how I feel about most of adulthood!

–Miss McD

Section 2: Comparing Fractions

Now that you've become an expert at identifying and creating equivalent fractions, it's time to put this new knowledge to work by comparing fractions that have different denominators. Comparing fractions helps us understand how values relate to each other and helps us make smart choices in everyday life, from figuring out who has more pizza to knowing who has the greatest slice of pie! We'll start by using simple benchmarks (fractions like 1/2) to quickly decide which fraction is greater or less. Next, we'll use the important skill of finding common denominators to compare fractions precisely. To make comparing fractions fun and memorable, you'll meet Slater, Numberock's fraction-loving alligator, who always chomps down on the greater fraction!

Learning Goals

I can (students will) compare two fractions with unlike denominators using benchmark fractions, common denominators, and geometric models, then record their findings with inequality symbols (<, >, =).

Teacher Tip

When you're teaching fraction comparison, visual tools like number lines and fraction models are essential. Demonstrating how fractions like 1/3 can become 2/6, and how that helps us compare it to fractions like 1/2 (3/6), clarifies abstract ideas. Remember to emphasize to your students that comparing fractions makes sense only when the wholes are the same size. For example, 1/2 of a small pizza might be less pizza than 1/4 of a giant pizza!

Whole Brain Learning Activity

As students watch Numberock's "Comparing Fractions" video, encourage them to mimic Slater the alligator's choices:

- When the greater fraction is on the right side of the screen, students should extend their arms to the right and "chomp" together.
- When the greater fraction appears on the left side, students "chomp" to the left.
- When fractions are equal, students form an equal sign by aligning their forearms horizontally.

This interactive, kinesthetic strategy helps solidify the concept and ensures students recall inequality symbols with ease.

Lesson: Comparing Fractions

Duration: 15–20 minutes

Intro

Students can use their understanding of benchmark fractions, same numerators, and same denominators to help them with comparing fractions! The butterfly method (cross multiplication) can also be used to determine which fraction is larger and which is smaller.

VIP Vocabulary

- Fraction: A way to represent a part of a whole
- Numerator: The top number in a fraction that shows how many parts we have
- Denominator: The bottom number in a fraction, the one that shows how many equal parts the whole is divided into
- Comparing Fractions: Determining which of two fractions is larger or smaller
- Benchmark Fraction: A "helper fraction," one that makes it easier to compare other fractions. Think of it as a fraction that you already know well and can use to see if other fractions are bigger, smaller, or about the same

---

Let's Rock!

Now's a great time to play Numberock's "Comparing Fractions" song!

Comparing Fractions For Kids Song

Comparing Fractions
https://numberock.com/mttm/

Questions Before, During, and After the Song

Before: How do you use symbols like < or > when comparing whole numbers? How might this be similar to using them when comparing fractions?

During: Pause at 0:52: Why does Slater the alligator choose to eat 5/6 instead of 2/6?

After: Use Slater the alligator's strategy to compare the fractions 3/4 and 5/8. Explain your reasoning.

Same Numerator

- Do: Draw two equal-sized rectangles on the board. Divide one into 5 parts and the other into 8 parts. Shade in one part of each.
- Ask: "If two fractions have the same numerator, how can we tell which one is greater and which is less?"
- Say: "When two fractions have the same numerator, we look at the denominator to help us. Remember, the larger the denominator, the smaller the part. Since 5 is a smaller number than 8, fifths are bigger than eighths. So 1/5 is greater than 1/8.
- Ask: "How can a model help prove or disprove our thinking?"

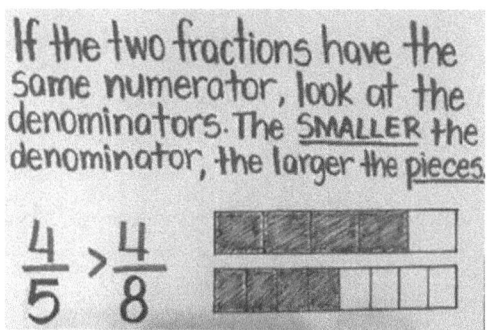

Watch me teach it here:

PRO TIP Use hand motions to show "The BIGGER the denominator, the SMALLER the part!" to help students lock it in!

Let's Practice!

- Ask: "What happens if I change the numerators to a number greater than 1? Will that change how we compare the fractions?"
- Do: Using the models from example 1, shade in four parts instead of one. Have students name the new fractions.
- Say: "Now we are comparing 4/5 and 4/8. Since the numerators are still the same, how can we decide which is smaller and which is larger?" Look at the denominators.
- Ask: "Which one is the greater fraction?" It is still 4/5 because fifths are larger than eighths.

    Partner Practice: Jamie has 2/3 of his homework left to do. His brother, Jerome, has 2/5 left to complete. Who has less homework to finish?

Same Denominator

- Do: Draw two equal-sized rectangles on the board. Divide both into 5 parts. Shade 4 parts of one and 2 parts of the other.
- Ask: "If two fractions have the same denominator, how can we tell which fraction is greater and which is less?"
- Say: "When two fractions have the same denominator, we look at the numerators to help us. Remember, the greater the numerator, the more parts are shaded. Since 4 is a larger number than 2, 4/5 is greater than 2/5.
- Ask: "How can a model help prove or disprove our thinking?"

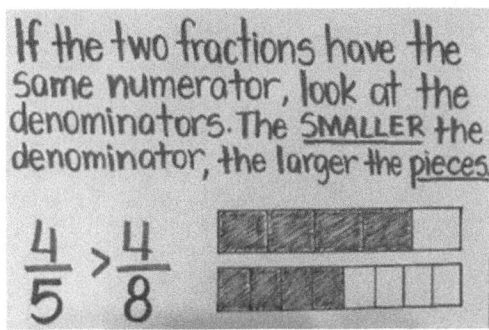

Watch me teach it here:

PRO TIP Have students chant, "Same denominator, see which numerator's greater!"

Let's Practice!

- Say: "Imagine we have two chocolate bars. Both are divided into 10 pieces. You eat 7 pieces of your bar, and your sister eats 5 pieces of her bar. How can we decide which is the greater amount eaten?" Follow-up hint: "Look at the numerator."
- Ask: "Which fraction is greater?" Answer: 7/10.

Partner Practice: "Isabella ran 5/8 of a mile during track practice. Lenny ran 3/8 of a mile. Who ran less? How do you know?"

Using Benchmarks to Compare

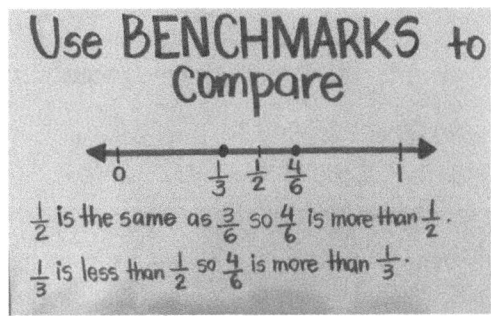

- Say: "Imagine you have a favorite toy that you use to measure other toys. If your favorite toy is 10 inches long, you can use it to see if other toys are longer, shorter, or about the same length. A benchmark fraction works the same way! We can use a number line with benchmark fractions such as 0, 1/4, 1/3, 1/2, 2/3, 3/4, and 1 to help us compare other fractions."
- Do: Draw a number line on the board. Have students label what they consider "benchmark fractions."
- Ask: "How can we use benchmark fractions to compare 2/5 and 7/10? Which benchmark fractions should we use?" Have students discuss their rationale for where the fraction should go on the number line compared to 0, 1/2, and 1.

Partner Practice: "Brayden used 3/6 of a yard of ribbon for his project. Maria used 6/8. How can you use benchmark fractions to decide who used the greater amount of ribbon?"

Butterfly Method (Cross-Multiplication)

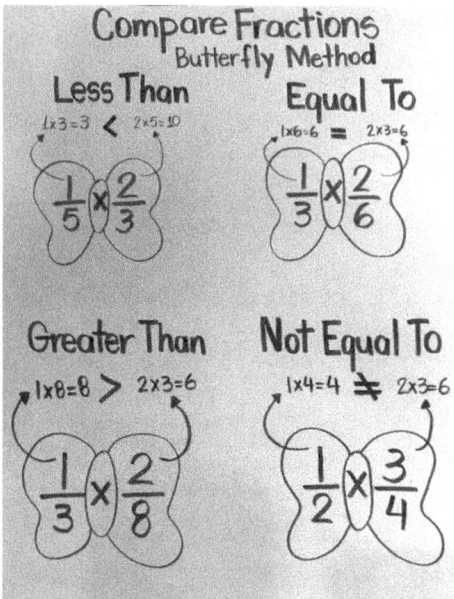

Students can use cross-multiplication (otherwise known as the butterfly method) to self-check their thinking, just as they did with finding equivalent fractions. Simply multiply the digits across from each other in the butterfly wings. If one product is larger, that fraction is larger!

Connect It!

"Fractions are abundant in everyday life. When would you need to compare them?"

- Example 1 – Restaurants/Bakeries: Chefs and bakers need to know if they have enough ingredients. If a recipe calls for 1/2 cup of flour and they have 2/3 cup of flour, comparing fractions will help them know if they need to go buy more or if they have enough in the store!
- Example 2 – Traveling: When you're taking a road trip, it's super important to know which gas station or rest stop is closer! If one is 4 1/2 miles away and the other is 4 3/8 miles away, you want to go to the one that is nearest. Comparing fractions will help you solve that problem!
- Other examples: Money, construction measurements, cutting up pizzas and other foods, supplies.

Team Talk: "Discuss places where you've had to compare fractions." Have students share, and don't forget to add their responses to your anchor chart!

Hands-On Activity: Fraction War

Objective

Students will use playing cards to create fractions and decide which ones are greater or less than the fractions their partners have on their cards!

Materials

Playing cards (you might need several decks depending on how many students are playing), fraction bars (to check for accuracy), and either whiteboards and markers or paper and pencil

Prep

Take out cards 2–10 in each suit of the cards. Put the rest to the side (you will not need them for this game!). Place students in pairs or small groups and pass out one bag of fraction bars or fraction circles per group. Give each pair/group of students a set of cards numbered 2–10 (the suit doesn't matter!).

Game Rules

- **Round 1: Beat Your Partner (5 minutes)**
  - Each person draws 2 cards from the deck and makes a proper fraction. For example, partner 1 pulls a 5 and a 2. Their fraction would be 2/5. Partner 2 pulls a 3 and a 9. Their fraction would be 3/9.
  - Students can use any strategy to decide which fraction is greater. The person with the larger fraction is the winner of that round. Reshuffle the cards and continue in round 2!

- **Round 2: Beat the Teacher (5 minutes)**
  - The teacher writes a fraction on the board (like 3/5) and the word "greater" OR the words "less than." Students have 1 minute to use their cards to create as many fractions with their cards (proper fractions only) that match the directions on the board. Discuss as a class and write the fractions on the board to check with the butterfly method.

Guided Practice

1. "Compare 2/6 and 5/6:

   Step 1: Identify common denominators (both fractions already have denominators of 6).
   Step 2: Compare numerators: 2 is less than 5, so 2/6 < 5/6."

2. "Compare 3/4 and 2/3 by finding common denominators:

   Step 1: Find a common denominator: 3/4 = 9/12 and 2/3 = 8/12.
   Step 2: Compare numerators: 9 is greater than 8, so 3/4 > 2/3."

3. Compare 5/8 and 3/10 by finding common denominators:

   Step 1: Find a common denominator: 5/8 = 25/40 and 3/10 = 12/40.
   Step 2: Compare numerators: 25 is greater than 12, so 5/8 > 3/10.

Practice Questions

Name/Date _____

Fill in the Blanks

1. 1/4 is _____ than 3/4.
2. To compare fractions easily, find a common _____.
3. Slater the alligator always eats the fraction that is _____.

Multiple Choice

1. Choose the correct inequality: 2/5 ____ 2/3

   A. >

   B. <

   C. =

2. Which fraction will Slater the alligator eat?

   A. 4/10

   B. 3/5

3. Which fraction equals 1/2?

   A. 2/4

   B. 2/5

   C. 3/4

Short Answer

1. Explain how the benchmark fraction 1/2 can help you quickly compare 3/7 and 3/5.

_____

_____

_____

2. How can you determine if fractions like 4/8 and 1/2 are equivalent?

_____

_____

_____

3. Why is finding a common denominator helpful for comparing fractions?

_____

_____

_____

Open Response

Draw and use geometric models to explain clearly how to compare the fractions 2/3 and 2/5.

Exit Ticket

1. Which symbol correctly compares 5/6 and 5/8? Explain clearly how you arrived at your answer.

_____

_____

_____

2. Write an inequality to compare 3/4 and 2/4. Describe how you know your inequality is correct.

_____

_____

_____

NUMBER AND OPERATIONS: FRACTIONS

05 Operations with Fractions

Notes from the Classroom

I was conducting math walk-throughs at an elementary school. The Assistant Principal and I walked into a fifth-grade classroom, and the students were excited to tell me what they were learning. Everyone crowded around me as one student exclaims, "We are learning about Dolly Parton fractions!"

It took me a moment ... but I finally realized they were learning about improper fractions (the top is bigger than the bottom!). I did ask the AP to talk to the teacher about using "proper" math language.

–Sandra Spicer

Section 1: Adding and Subtracting Fractions with Like Denominators

Adding or subtracting fractions with the same denominator hinges on one simple idea: the denominator (the size of each slice) never changes, only the number of slices does. Begin by inviting students to recall moments they've shared pizza, pie, or chocolate. These are all real-life fractions that spark curiosity. Offer manipulatives such as fraction bars, pattern blocks, or even paper cut-outs so learners can combine or remove equal parts. Once they've got used to the concrete, guide them to visualize operations on number lines and area models. Finally, anchor their understanding with the equation format. To help students remember the process, Numberock's catchy song "Adding Fractions with Like Denominators" reminds students that "The bottoms don't budge—they're steady and sane—but those wacky numerators just love to play games!"

Learning Goals

I can (students will) use real-world scenarios, hands-on models, and equations to add and subtract fractions with like denominators.

Teacher Tip

Activate students' prior knowledge by reminding them that a fraction names equal parts of a whole. Emphasize that when you combine (or remove) like pieces (quarters, eighths, sixths), the denominator, which tells us the size of each part, remains unchanged. Clarify that they are simply joining or separating pieces of the same size, so only the numerator shifts.

Whole Brain Teaching

Enhance memory by pairing movement with melody. Have students act out the lyrics:

1. "To add or subtract fractions with the same denominator": arms extend horizontally to form a bar in front of them.

2. "Same denominator": hands drop down and fold together to show two equal denominators.

3. "In the sum or difference, it stays the same": forearms cross for "+," and one forearm is held out horizontally for "−."

4. "We only add or subtract each numerator": students raise each hand above their heads to represent the numerators.

5. "And the answer will be ours to proclaim!": cup hands around the mouth and call out with enthusiasm.

Lesson: Adding and Subtracting Fractions with Like Denominators

Duration: 15–20 minutes

Intro

Relating fractions to food is a great way to get buy-in from students (it's relatable and they seem to always be hungry! Lol!). I always ask them to think about sharing their favorite treat with their friends and using either real treats (depending on what your school allows!) or counters to represent them.

VIP Vocabulary

- Fraction: A way to represent a part of a whole, written as a/b, where "a" is the numerator and "b" is the denominator.
- Numerator: The top number in a fraction, the number that shows how many parts we have.
- Denominator: The bottom number in a fraction, the number that shows how many equal parts the whole is divided into.
- Like Denominators: When two fractions have the same denominator, we say that the two fractions share "like denominators."

Adding Fractions with Like Denominators

- Do: Draw 12 circles on the board. These represent the number of treats in the bag that the students will be sharing today.
- Ask: "If you gave your best friend 3 of the treats, what fraction of the whole does that represent?" Answer: 3/12. "If I ate four of the treats, what fraction of the whole does that represent?" Answer: 4/12.
- Say: "Out of the bag of treats, we've used 3/12 and 4/12. To figure out the total fraction of treats that are gone from the bag now, we can either add or subtract those fractions. What operation would we use here?" Answer: Addition.
- Do: Shade in 3 circles with one color and 4 circles with another color to represent the two fractions.
- Ask: "What is the fraction represented on the board now that 7 circles are shaded in?" Answer: 7/12. "What did you notice about the numerator and denominators of our original fractions?" Answer: The numerators got added; the denominator stayed the same. "Why didn't the denominator change?"

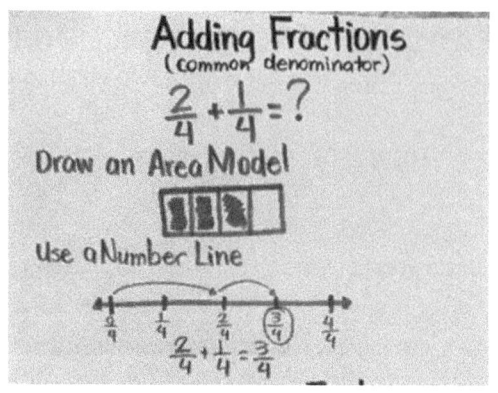

Watch me teach it here:

PRO TIP Use this rhyme to help students remember NOT to add the denominators (a common misconception!). "**Numerators add, they're on top. Denominator stays, so you STOP!**"

Let's Rock!

Now's a great time to play Numberock's "Adding Fractions with Like Denominators Numbers" song!

Adding Fractions with Like Denominators Numbers	
https://numberock.com/mttm/	

Questions Before, During, and After the Song

Before: "Recall a time when you shared food like pizza, pie, or candy and needed to find out how much was left or combined. How would you represent that with fractions?"

During: "In verse 1 of the song, two eighths of pizza are eaten. How many eighths remain, and why does the denominator stay eight?"

After: "Verse 2 describes saving two slices of pie cut into fourths. What fraction of the pie has been saved? Explain your thinking."

Subtracting Fractions with Like Denominators

- Do: Refer students back to the example on the board. Put an x through the 7 circles shaded in Problem 1.
- Ask: "We're going to use the last problem to help us solve a new one. Since some of the treats are gone, what operation should we use to see how many are left? (subtract)
- Say: "7/12 of the treats are gone. To figure out what fraction of treats are left, we need to know the fraction of treats we started with. What fraction is one whole bag of treats? (12/12)
- Do: Shade in the remaining 5 circles with a different color.
- Ask: "What is the fraction represented on the board now that there are only 5 circles remaining? (5/12) What did you notice about the numerator and denominators of our original fractions? (the numerators got subtracted, the denominator stayed the same). Why didn't the denominator change?"

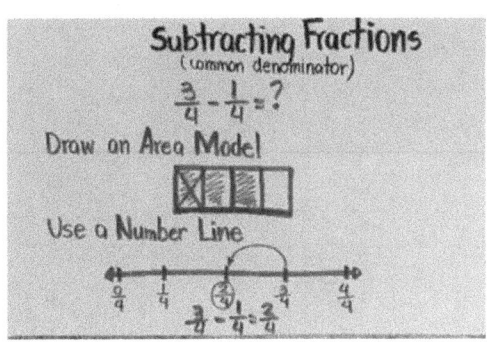

PRO TIP This is a great time to repeat the rhyme "**Numerators subtract, they're on top. Denominator stays, so you STOP!**" Remind students that just like in subtraction with whole numbers, the larger fraction always comes first in the problem.

Watch me teach it here:

Adding Mixed Numbers (Like Denominators)

Intro

This skill builds on the previous understanding of adding and subtracting fractions with like denominators but adds on with regrouping.

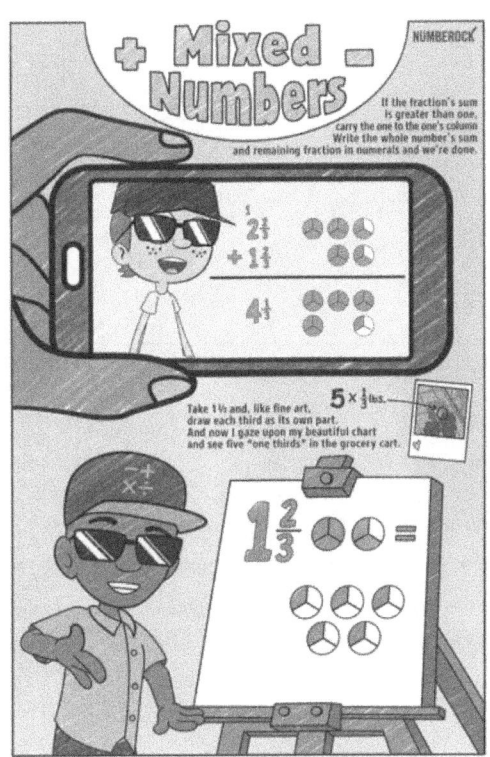

Let's Rock!

Now's a great time to play Numberock's "Adding Mixed Numbers" Song.

Adding Mixed Numbers	
https://numberock.com/mttm/	

Questions Before, During, and After the Song

Before: How is a mixed number different from an improper fraction?

During: (pause around the 0:57 mark) Should you rewrite these mixed numbers as improper fractions or leave as mixed numbers? Which is better? (pause around 2:10) What do we do when the fractional sum is greater than 1? (regroup)

After: Why is it okay to only add fractional parts when denominators are the same? How would the process change if denominators were different? (preparing for future learning)

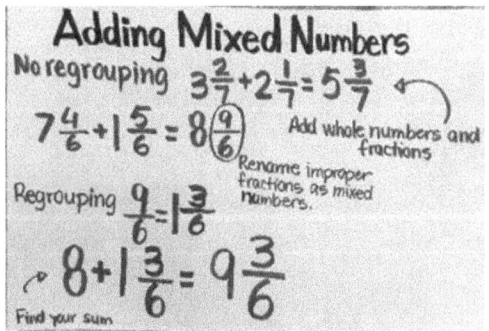

Watch me teach it here:

PRO TIP Regrouping with fractions is the same as regrouping with whole numbers. When the place value is full (for fractions it means we've reached one whole!), it has to be regrouped into the ones place! The remaining fraction stays in the **fraction's place.**

Subtracting Mixed Numbers (Like Denominators)

Intro

This skill builds on the previous understanding of adding and subtracting fractions with like denominators but adds on with regrouping.

PRO TIP Reflect on subtracting with whole numbers and when it's necessary to group!

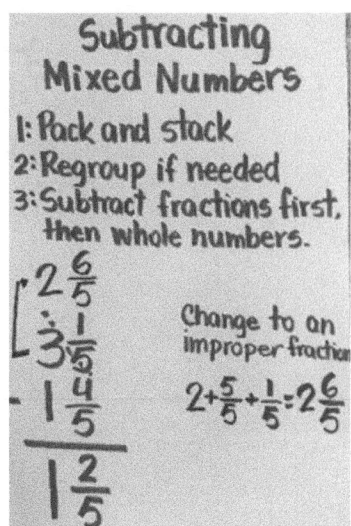

Watch me teach it here:

Let's Rock – ENRICHMENT!

Now's a great time to play Numberock's "Adding and Subtracting Fractions" song! This song is for fourth graders ready to be exposed to unlike denominators.

"Adding & Subtracting Fractions Song" by NUMBEROCK

Adding and Subtracting Fractions	
https://numberock.com/mttm/	

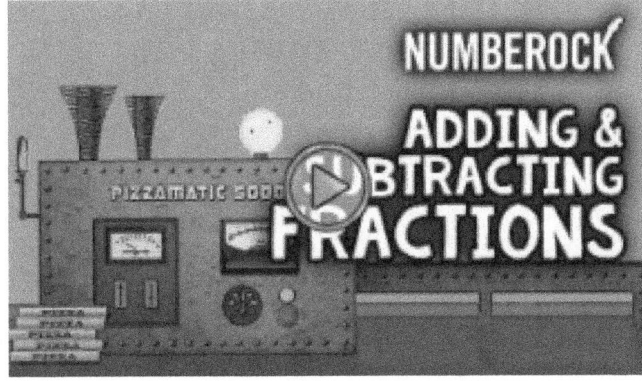

Questions Before, During, and After the Song

Before: How could we add or subtract fractions that don't have the same denominator? What challenges might there be?

During: (pause around 1:40) What transformations are they doing to the fractions so that denominators match?

How does the rhyme and repetition of the song help you remember the steps?

After: Can you create your own word problem where you add two fractions with unlike denominators?

Watch me teach it here:

Connect It!

"Adding and subtracting fractions is a daily part of life – let's look at some examples!"

- Example 1 – Cooking: Making multiple batches of a recipe or cutting a batch in 1/2
- Example 2 – Gardening: Watering 3/8 of the garden in the morning and figuring how much you have to water in the afternoon
- Other examples: Sports (how points are split during a game), traveling (how far you've gone and how far there still is to go), homework

Team Talk: "Discuss places where you've seen fractions being added or subtracted." Have students share, and don't forget to add their responses to your anchor chart!

Hands-On Activity: Planning a Picnic

Duration: 5–10 minutes

Materials

- Paper
- Pencils
- Colored markers

Intro

"You're going on a picnic! You'll need to calculate how much of each item you have in the picnic basket and how much is left over when you're done eating!"

Activity Steps

Step 1:   Provide the students with the following information on the board:

- Juice: Each bottle contains 3/4 of a liter. They have 3 bottles.
- Sandwiches: Each sandwich is cut into 1/2 pieces. They have 5 pieces.
- Fruit: Each fruit bowl contains 2/3 of a kilogram. They have 4 bowls.

Step 2:   Ask the students to add the fractions to find the total quantities:

- Juice: 3/4 + 3/4 + 3/4 = 9/4 or 2 1/4 liters
- Sandwiches: 1/2 + 1/2 + 1/2 + 1/2 + 1/2 = 5/2 or 2 1/2 sandwiches
- Fruit: 2/3 + 2/3 + 2/3 + 2/3 = 8/3 or 2 2/3 kilograms

Step 3:   Have the students draw the picnic items and label the quantities with their fractions.

Step 4:   Have the students decide how much of each juice, sandwiches, and fruit has been consumed during the picnic. Mark an "×" on each item eaten/drunk, and have students write a subtraction equation to match their model.

Have a gallery walk to share student thinking and proudly post their work around the room!

Guided Practice

1. "Layla's sub sandwich was cut into six equal pieces. She ate 2 at lunch and 1 at dinner. How much did she eat?

   Add the numerators: 2 + 1 = 3.

   Keep the denominator, 6.

   Answer: 3/6 of the sandwich."

2. "Jacob had 5/8 of a chocolate bar and shared 2/8 with his sister. How much remains?

   Subtract the numerators: 5 − 2 = 3.

   Denominator remains 8.

   Answer: 3/8 remains."

3. "A dog ate 1/4 of a treat in the morning and 2/4 in the afternoon. How much did the dog eat?

   Add the numerators: 1 + 2 = 3.

   Denominator stays 4.

   Answer: 3/4 of the treat."

Practice Questions

Name/Date _____

Fill in the Blanks

1. When adding fractions with like denominators, we add only the _____.

2. The _____ stays the same when we add or subtract like fractions.

3. 2/6 + 3/6 = _____.

Multiple Choice

1. 3/5 + 1/5 = ?

   A. 4/10

   B. 4/5

   C. 3/10

   D. 5/5

2. Why doesn't the denominator change when you add fractions with like denominators?

   A. Because it's easier.

   B. Because numerators are smaller.

   C. Because the size of the parts stays the same.

   D. Because the result must be a whole.

3. 6/7 − 2/7 = ?

   A. 4/7

   B. 3/5

   C. 6/5

   D. 8/7

Short Answer

1. Explain why 3/4 + 1/4 = 4/4.

_____

_____

_____

2. If you eat 2/8 of a pie and your friend eats 3/8, how much of the pie have you eaten together?

_____

_____

_____

3. Why don't we add denominators when adding like fractions?

_____

_____

_____

Open Response

Ben and Mia are baking pies. Ben eats 1/6 and Mia eats 4/6 of the same pie. Do they finish it?

_____

_____

_____

_____

_____

_____

Exit Ticket

1. 5/9 – 3/9 = _____

2. In your own words, describe what stays the same when you add or subtract fractions with like denominators and why.

_____

_____

_____

Notes from the Classroom

One of my cutest stories was during the time I was getting my teacher license, and I was subbing in a kindergarten class. I told the kids "My name is Mrs. Kinner," and then added, "it rhymes with dinner (so they wouldn't forget it) and NOBODY forgets dinner!"

Throughout the day the kids would call me either Mrs. Kinner or Mrs. Dinner. I answered to both.

A couple weeks later I saw one of the kindergartners at the grocery store. She looked surprised to see me there and turned to her mother and said, "Look! It's Mrs. Cook! She must live here!" Her mother and I got a big laugh out of that! What a great place for Mrs. Cook Dinner to live – in a grocery store!

–Debbie Kinner

Section 2: Multiplying Fractions by Whole Numbers

Students have mastered multiplying whole numbers and explored the world of fractions, but now it's time to bring those ideas together. Multiplying a whole number by a fraction is simply another way to ask, "What part of an amount do we have?" We'll start with concrete examples like area models, number lines, and repeated addition so that students see and feel what's happening. Once that foundation is solid, we introduce the efficient two-step algorithm of "multiply by the top, divide by the bottom," which will be reinforced through Numberock's song and examples.

Learning Goals

I can (students will) multiply whole numbers by fractions using visual models, repeated addition, and the standard algorithm.

Teacher Tip

Anchor this lesson in familiar contexts. For example, show a video of a runner covering 3/4 of an 8-mile course (8 × 3 ÷ 4 = 6 miles). Or slice a pizza into fourths: three slices represent 3 × 1/4, the same as 3/4. Discussing "pizza fractions" and "miles run" helps students connect abstract procedures to the world they know.

Whole Brain Teaching

As the song's chorus repeats "Multiply by the top, divide by the bottom," guide students through a simple dance routine to solidify each step in memory. Have them cross their forearms in an "×" and pump their fist on "multiply by the top," then make a diagonal down-slash motion on "divide by the bottom." These coordinated movements engage kinesthetic, auditory, and visual pathways, making the algorithm unforgettable.

Lesson: Multiplying Fractions by Whole Numbers

Duration: 15–20 minutes

Intro

This standard includes a couple different types of multiplying fractions: multiplying a whole number by a fraction and multiplying fractions by a whole number.

VIP Vocabulary

- Fraction: A way to represent a part of a whole, written as a/b, where "a" is the numerator and "b" is the denominator
- Numerator: The top number in a fraction, the one that shows how many parts we have
- Denominator: The bottom number in a fraction, the one that shows how many equal parts the whole is divided into
- Product: The result of multiplying two numbers

Multiplying a Whole Number by a Fraction (Models)

Remind students that the "×" sign means "groups of." When we are multiplying a whole number by a fraction, we are making groups of a fraction and can solve using repeated addition!

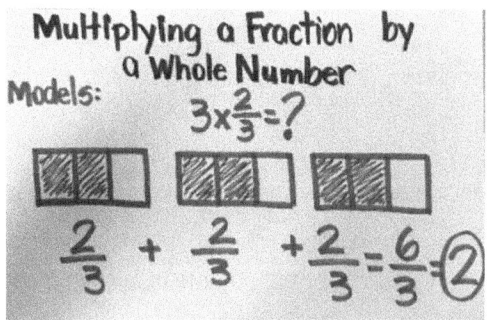

- Do: Draw a rectangle to represent the fraction 2/3. Have students create a scenario to represent the model. For example, "I ate 2/3 of my candy bar on Monday."
- Ask: "What happens if I repeat this action on multiple days? How do I show more than one group of 2/3? What operation do we use to show repeated addition?" Answer: Multiplication.
- Do: Draw an additional rectangle representing 2/3. Ask students to solve using repeated addition. The rectangle should show that 2/3 + 2/3 = 4/3.

TO SOLVE $\frac{3}{4}$ × 8 BY MULTIPLYING:

STEP ONE: MULTIPLY THE WHOLE NUMBER BY THE NUMERATOR.

$$\frac{3}{4} \times 8 = \frac{(3 \times 8)}{4} = \frac{24}{4}$$

STEP TWO: DIVIDE THE NUMERATOR BY THE DENOMINATOR.

$$\frac{24}{4} = 24 / 4 = 6$$

- Ask: "How can we represent this problem using multiplication? What is 2 groups of 2/3?" Answer: 2 × 2/3. "Repeat adding additional rectangles with 2/3 in each."

Multiplying a Fraction by a Whole Number (Models)

When we multiply a fraction by a whole number, we are taking a PART of the original number, so our product is going to be LESS than the whole we started with. This is a great way for students to double-check their answers by ensuring they end up with less than they started with!

- Say: "We're going to use the same problem from example 1, but observe what happens when we swap the factors. Remember, "×" means "groups of" or "of." If we swap the 3 and 2/3, our new problem will be 2/3 × 3. This means I'm starting with 3 wholes, and I'm taking 2/3 of that amount.
- Do: Draw the rectangle from example 1 (cut into thirds), with no parts shaded.
- Ask: "If we are starting with 3 parts, how much is 1 out of 3, or 1/3?" Answer: 1 part would be shaded. "So, if we are trying to find 2 out of 3 parts or 2/3 of 3, how many parts will be shaded?" Answer: 2 parts would be shaded.

Let's Rock!

Now's a great time to play Numberock's "Multiplying Fractions by Whole Numbers" Video

Multiplying Fractions by Whole Numbers	
https://numberock.com/mttm/	

"Multiplying Fractions by Whole Numbers Song" with Word Problems

MULTIPLYING FRACTIONS BY WHOLE NUMBERS

TO SOLVE $\frac{3}{4} \times 8$ BY MULTIPLYING:

STEP ONE: MULTIPLY the WHOLE NUMBER by the NUMERATOR

$$\frac{3}{4} \times 8 = \frac{(3 \times 8)}{4} = \frac{24}{4}$$

STEP TWO: DIVIDE the NUMERATOR by the DENOMINATOR

$$\frac{24}{4} = 24 / 4 = 6$$

Questions Before, During, and After the Song

Before: "What does multiplying a fraction like 3/4 by 8 represent in real life? Can you name a situation where you'd calculate a fraction of a quantity (e.g., recipe measurements, running, or sharing)?"

During: "The song shows 12 × 5 ÷ 6 = 10. Why do we multiply by the numerator (top) first, then divide by the denominator (bottom)?"

After: "The song uses repeated addition to solve 1/2 × 3. Now try 2/3 × 6 with both repeated addition and the algorithm. Do they match?"

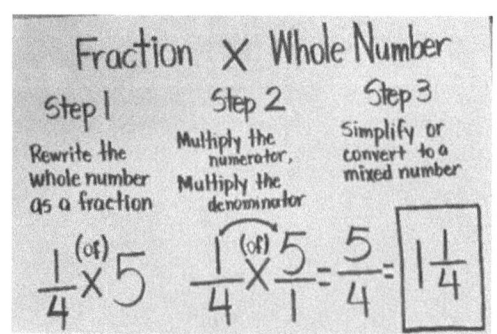

PRO TIP Remember the lyrics "Multiply by the top, Divide by the bottom!"

Watch me teach it here:

Connect It!

"Multiplying fractions is a daily part of life – let's look at some examples!"

- Example 1 – Cooking: Making multiple batches of a recipe or cutting a batch in 1/2. If one batch of cookies uses 1/2 cup of chocolate chips and you want to make 3 batches, you need to multiply 3 by 1/2. So, 3 × 1/2 = 3/2, which is the same as 1 and 1/2 cups of chocolate chips.
- Example 2 – Exercising: If you run 3/4 of a mile each day and you want to know how far you run in 5 days, you need to multiply 3/4 by 5. So, 5 × 3/4 = 15/4, which is the same as 3 and 3/4 miles.
- Other examples: Budgeting, traveling, completion of homework and chores.

   Team Talk: "Discuss places where you've seen fractions being multiplied." Have students share, and don't forget to add their responses to your anchor chart!

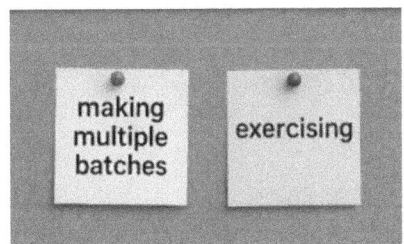

Hands-On Activity: Baking Cookies

Duration: 5–10 minutes

Materials

- Paper
- Pencils
- Colored markers (optional)

Intro

"Today you are going to help adjust a cookie recipe so you can make multiple batches! You need to figure out the quantities of ingredients required using your knowledge of multiplying fractions."

Activity Steps

Step 1: Provide the students with the basic cookie recipe:

- Flour: 3/4 cup
- Sugar: 1/2 cup
- Butter: 1/3 cup

Step 2: Ask the students to decide how many cookies they want to make. For example, if the original recipe makes 12 cookies, they might want to make 24 cookies (double the recipe) or 36 cookies (triple the recipe).

Step 3: Have the students multiply the fractions to adjust the recipe:

BAKING COOKIES
Multiply Fractions to plan the quantities of ingredients

- Doubling the Recipe (24 cookies):
- Flour: 2 × 3/4 = 6/4 or 1 1/2 cups
- Sugar: 2 × 1/2 = 2/2 or 1 cup
- Butter: 2 × 1/3 = 2/3 cups
- Tripling the Recipe (36 cookies):
- Flour: 3 × 3/4 = 9/4 or 2 1/4 cups
- Sugar: 3 × 1/2 = 3/2 or 1 1/2 cups
- Butter: 3 × 1/3 = 3/3 cups or 1 cup

Step 4: Have the students draw the ingredients and label the quantities with their fractions.

Enrichment: Have students try to halve the recipe! Multiply each quantity by 1/2 to begin working with multiplying fractions by fractions.

Guided Practice

1. "Compute 3 × 1/4
   Repeated addition: 1/4 + 1/4 + 1/4 = 3/4
   Algorithm: 3 × 1 = 3, 3 ÷ 4 = 3/4"

2. "Compute 2 × 5/6
   Multiply by numerator: 2 × 5 = 10
   Divide by denominator: 10 ÷ 6 = 10/6 = 1 4/6 = 1 2/3"

3. "Compute 4 × 3/8
   Multiply by numerator: 4 × 3 = 12
   Divide by denominator: 12 ÷ 8 = 1 4/8 = 1 1/2"

Practice Questions

Name/Date _____

Fill in the Blanks

1. To multiply a whole number by a fraction, first multiply the _____ by the numerator.

2. Then divide your product by the _____.

3. 4 × 1/2 equals _____.

Multiple Choice

1. Which phrase describes the correct steps?

   A. Multiply by the bottom, then divide by the top

   B. Multiply by the top, then divide by the bottom

   C. Multiply top and bottom together

2. What is 3 × 1/3?

   A. 3/3   B. 1/3   C. 3/9

3. What is 5 × 2/5?

   A. 2   B. 1   C. 5

Short Answer

1. Describe how 1/2 × 6 can be solved using both repeated addition and the algorithm.

   _____

   _____

   _____

2. Use a visual model (like a pizza or number line) to show what 3 × 1/2 means.

3. How does "multiply by the top, divide by the bottom" serve as an effective strategy?

_____

_____

_____

Open Response

Solve 3 × 2/5 using a visual model (area model or number line) and the algorithm. Show your steps and explain how both methods confirm your answer.

Exit Ticket

1. Use the song's method to solve 5 × 3/4 = _____?

2. A runner completes 2/3 of a 9-mile trail. How many miles did they run?

_____

_____

_____

06 Decimals and Fractions

Notes from the Classroom

A few years ago, I had 3 girls in my class named Ashley, all spelled differently of course! All three had unique personalities, and all were good students.

We were learning fact families, using manipulatives, everyone was really into the lesson. I stopped the action for a quick check for understanding, thumbs up or down to show if they agreed or disagreed with the summary statement I made. Every student had the correct response quickly, so I knew we could move forward.

Suddenly Danny, who often struggled with math, raised his hand and shouted, "Oh! Now I get it!" I was excited for him, so I asked him to put into his own words his new understanding of fact families. "No, not that," he said. "Now I know how to tell the Ashleys apart—Ashley N is the mean one!"

Not the response I was looking for, but he was not wrong! It did all add up! He learned a different kind of math that day!

–Jill Swann

Section 1: Understanding Decimals and Fractions

In this section we will explore how fractions with denominators of 10, 100, and 1,000 are expressed as decimals. Students will see that these denominators are special because they are powers of ten. We will use number lines, area models, and grids to visualize how these fractions can be represented as decimals. Students will also connect their learning to contexts such as money and measurement. Finally, we will learn how to record decimal fractions on place value charts and reinforce the lesson with Numberock's "Relating Fractions to Decimals" song.

Learning Goals

I can (students will) understand the equivalence between fractions with denominators of 10, 100, and 1,000 and their decimal forms and be able to convert between fractions and decimals and compare them.

Whole Brain Teaching

During the chorus when the lyrics say "Whole numbers to the left," have students punch to the left with their left hand. When they hear "Decimals to the right," they punch to the right with their right hand. As the song continues, "They get smaller and smaller till they're barely in sight," students take steps to the right while crouching lower toward the ground. This movement helps reinforce how decimals become smaller and smaller parts as we move right on the place value chart.

Lesson: Relating Decimals to Fractions

Duration: 15–20 minutes

Intro

Relating fractions to decimals is so much easier to understand when it's connected to . . . MONEY! When students understand that tenths are like dimes and hundredths are like pennies, they can concretely connect the two values.

VIP Vocabulary

- Decimal: A number that shows a part of a whole, written with a decimal point (e.g., 0.5)
- Fraction: A way to represent a part of a whole, written as a/b, where "a" is the numerator and "b" is the denominator
- Numerator: The top number in a fraction, the one that shows how many parts we have
- Denominator: The bottom number in a fraction, the one that shows how many equal parts the whole is divided into
- Equivalent: Having the same value or amount

This is a great lesson to start with a song! The Numberock lyrics and visuals are so helpful to build the foundation of how decimals are related to fractions. In this standard, we focus on tenths and hundredths only, but feel free to let kids explore thousandths and beyond as they are grappling with this concept!

Let's Rock!

Now's a great time to play Numberock's "Relating Fractions to Decimals" song! Decimals to Fractions Song | Decimal Notation

Relating Fractions to Decimals	
https://numberock.com/mttm/	

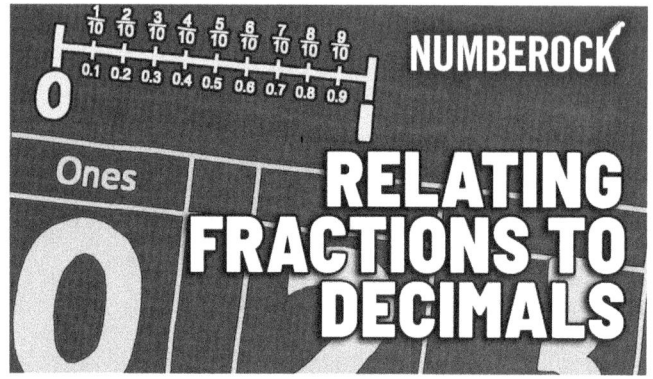

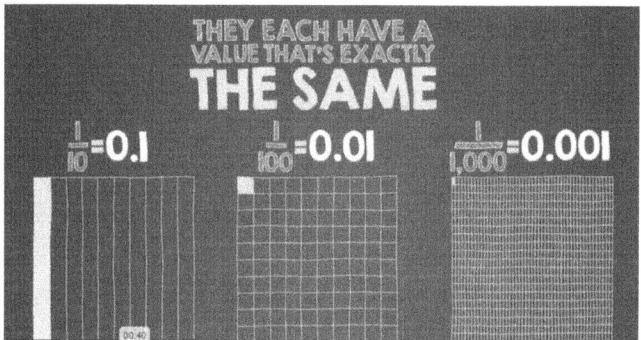

Questions Before, During, and After the Song

Before: "What do you think happens to a number's value when we move a digit one place to the left?"

During: Pause at 2:30: Why does the song say that there is a "special land between zero and one?"

After: "How would you explain to a friend why the 5 in 0.5 is worth ten times more than the 5 in 0.05?" Have your students pair up and have one student explain, with the other student reporting their partner's explanation back to the class.

Finding Equivalent Fractions/Decimals

(Grab penny and dime manipulatives if you have them!)

- Do: Draw a [grid]. Write 20¢ on the board. Ask students how that amount can be represented with dimes. Shade in the model or use manipulatives.
- Ask: "How can we represent this value as a fraction?" Answer: 2/10. "How can we represent this value as a decimal?" Answer: 0.2.

- Say: "Imagine we had only pennies to represent the same amount. How many pennies would we need to swap out for the two dimes?" Answer: 20. "How can we represent this as a decimal?" Answer: 0.20. "These decimals are equivalent and worth the same amount."
- Do: Write 2/10 and 20/100 on the board. Have students discuss how the fractions are the same.
- Ask: "How are 0.2 and 0.20 alike? How does the zero change the value of the decimal?"

Fractions and Decimals
Two ways to describe Parts of a Whole

Fraction	Decimal	Model	Number Line
$\frac{3}{10}$	0.3		
$\frac{35}{100}$	0.35		

One Whole   One-tenth   One-hundredths

$\frac{1}{1}$ $\frac{10}{10}$ $\frac{100}{100}$ $\frac{1}{10}$ 0.1 $\frac{1}{100}$ 0.01

PRO TIP A common error students make when finding equivalent fractions is adding a zero to the numerator and not the denominator. Remind students that when they find equivalent fractions, the numerator and denominator must both be multiplied by the same amount.

Watch me teach it here:

Let's Practice

$$\frac{5}{10} = \frac{50}{100}$$

$$\boxed{} = 0.50$$

$$\boxed{} = \frac{60}{100}$$

$$0.6 = 0.60$$

Connect It!

"Being able to see the connection between fractions and decimals is a super important life skill! Where else have you seen this connection?"

money   reading a ruler

- Example 1 – MONEY! Understanding that if you have 50 cents, you have 50/100 of a dollar, which is the same as $0.50. This is also the same as 5/10.
- Example 2 – Reading a Ruler: On a ruler, 1/10 of a centimeter is the same as 0.1 centimeter. This is also the same as 10/100 of a centimeter (0.10 centimeter).

    Team Talk: "Discuss places where you've seen fractions connected to decimals." Have students share, and don't forget to add their responses to your anchor chart!

Hands-On Activity: Open a Class Store

Duration: 10–15 minutes

Materials

- Paper
- Pencils
- Sticky notes or index cards

Set up: Have students choose 2 items from their desk or around the classroom to put in the school store, and price each item between $0.01 and $1.00 (adjust as needed for enrichment) on a sticky note.

Activity Steps
Introduction: "Today we're going to sell some of our classroom items and set up a class store. We'll need to figure out the prices of items using our knowledge of decimals and fractions."

1. Tell students they have $2.00 to go shopping with (adjust amount as needed).

2. As students choose an item to purchase, they must convert the decimal prices to fractions with denominators of 10 or 100:

   Example: Pencil: $0.30 = 30/100 = 3/10; Notebook: $0.54 = 54/100

3. Have students draw the items and label the prices with both decimals and fractions.

   Enrichment: Calculate the total amount spent in both decimals and fractions.

4. Have students present and share their purchases.

Discussion Questions:

- "What is the greatest number of items you could have purchased with your money at this store?"
- "Can you convert every decimal price to a fraction with a denominator out of 100? Out of 10? Why or why not?"

Guided Practice

1. Convert 7/10 to a decimal and show it on a number line.
   Step 1: Recognize that 7/10 means 7 parts out of 10. The decimal is 0.7.
   Step 2: Draw a number line from 0 to 1, divide it into 10 equal parts, and mark the seventh
      interval to show 0.7 = 7/10.
   Step 3: Relate this to money: 7/10 of a dollar is $0.70.

2. Express 3/10 as an equivalent fraction with denominator 100; then convert to a decimal.
   Step 1: Multiply numerator and denominator by 10 to get 30/100.
   Step 2: Convert 30/100 to 0.30 or 0.3.
   Step 3: Use a grid to show that 3/10 = 30/100 = 0.3.

3. Add 4/10 + 7/100 and write the sum as a decimal.
   Step 1: Convert 4/10 to 40/100.
   Step 2: Add 40/100 + 7/100 = 47/100.
   Step 3: Convert to decimal 0.47 and connect to measurement, such as 0.47 meters.

Practice Questions

Name/Date _____

Fill in the Blanks

1. The fraction 9/10 is equivalent to the decimal _____.

2. Write 0.25 as an equivalent fraction with denominator 100: _____/100.

3. 6/100 as a decimal is _____, and as an equivalent fraction with a
   denominator of 1000 it is _____/1,000.

Multiple Choice

1. Which decimal is equivalent to 45/100?

   A. 0.045   C. 4.5

   B. 0.45   D. 45.0

2. How would you express 7/10 as a fraction with denominator 100?

   A. 7/100   C. 700/100

   B. 70/100   D. 17/100

3. $0.50 is the same as which fraction?

   A. 50/10   C. 50/100

   B. 5/100   D. 500/100

Short Answer

1. Explain why 0.8 is the same as 8/10, and show this on a number line.

   _____

   _____

   _____

2. Convert 0.06 to a fraction and describe how it relates to money, such as cents in a dollar.

_____

_____

_____

3. Compare 3/10 and 25/100. Which is larger and why? Use equivalent fractions to explain.

_____

_____

_____

Open Response

Imagine you have a pizza divided into 100 equal slices and you eat 35 slices. Write this as a fraction and as a decimal. Then imagine you eat 3/10 of another pizza. Show how to add the two amounts using equivalent fractions and decimals.

_____

_____

_____

_____

_____

Exit Ticket

1. Convert 12/100 to a decimal and explain why they are equivalent.

_____

_____

_____

2. If 4/10 = 0.4, what is 4/100 as a decimal? Write your answer and connect it to an example such as length in meters.

_____

_____

_____

Notes from the Classroom

I teach new-to-country students how to speak English. It's so sweet how they pick up things. Days of the week are "Monday, Twosday, Threesday, Foursday, Fivesday!"

–Enn Emm See

Section 2: Comparing Decimals

In this section we are going to learn how to compare decimals by reasoning about place value. Students will line up decimals correctly, compare digits from left to right, and record their results with the symbols <, >, and =. We will also connect decimals to fractions and to examples such as money and number lines. The "Comparing Decimals" song introduces Slater the alligator, who always chomps the greater number, helping students remember the rules of comparison while making the lesson fun and memorable.

Learning Goals

I can (students will) compare two decimals up to the hundredths by reasoning about their size using place value, number lines, or visual models. I can (students will) record my (their) results with the symbols >, =, or < while recognizing that comparisons are valid only when referring to the same whole.

Teacher Tip

Introduce the alligator metaphor before playing the song. Explain that the alligator's mouth always opens toward the larger number. Begin with concrete examples such as money. For example, compare $0.55 and $0.65 to show that 65 cents is greater. Then move to showing decimals lined up vertically so students can compare place values more easily. Finally, move to abstract comparisons using inequality symbols. This progression helps students avoid common mistakes such as ignoring digits after the tenths place.

Whole Brain Learning

Bring the alligator to life with movement. During the chorus line "The hungry alligator eats the value that is greater," students form an alligator mouth with their arms and chomp toward the larger decimal displayed on the board. When the numbers are equal, students place their forearms in front of their bodies to make an equals sign. These movements reinforce symbols and place value while keeping students actively engaged.

Lesson: Comparing Decimals

Duration: 15–20 minutes

Intro

Understanding how to compare decimals can help students in situations such as reading prices, comparing grades, and understanding scores in sports, so this is a great unit to connect to their personal experiences! As with the last section, this standard focuses on comparing decimals up to the hundredths (but check out the thousandths for an extra challenge!).

VIP Vocabulary

- Decimal: A number that shows a part of a whole, written with a decimal point (e.g., 0.5)
- Place Value: The value of a digit based on its position in a number (e.g., tenths, hundredths)
- Greater Than (>): A symbol used to compare two numbers, indicating the first number is larger
- Less Than (<): A symbol used to compare two numbers, indicating the first number is smaller
- Equal To (=): A symbol used to show that two numbers are the same

---

Let's Rock!

Now's a great time to play Numberock's "Comparing Decimals" song!
Comparing Decimals Song

Comparing Decimals	
https://numberock.com/mttm/	

Comparing Decimals

(Grab penny and dime manipulatives if you have them!)

- Say: "Money is a great way to understand decimals. Every dollar is made of 100 cents, so $0.75 means 75 cents. If the whole number is the same, like in 2.30 and 2.03, we look at the tenths and hundredths to decide which is more. It's like comparing how much money you have – even a few cents can make a difference!"
- Do: Write two amounts on the board: 0.56 and 0.65 side by side. Ask students to help draw a model of both using and representing with place value disks or money. Have students assist with plotting the two decimals on a number line.

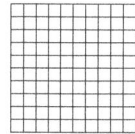

- Say: "Let's look at these models and discuss which is more. How does each model help us determine which has a greater value and which has less?"
- Do: Now line up the decimals by place value:
  0.56
  0.65
- Ask: Which place value do we need to look at to be able to compare the decimals? Answer: Tenths.
- Say: "Since 0.65 has 6 tenths and 0.56 has 5 tenths, 0.65 is GREATER THAN 0.56."

Let's Practice!

- Say: You're buying a toy that costs $4.75. You have $4.50. Do you have more or less than you need? How do you know?"

  "Look at these three prices: $3.25, $3.52, and $3.05. Can you put them in order from least to greatest? What strategy did you use?"

Comparing Decimals

Compare: 1.11 , 0.88 , 0.8

Make a Place Value chart

Ones	•	Tenths	Hundredths
1	•	1	1
0	•	8	8
0	•	8	0

(Fill in blank spaces with zeros)

1.11 > 0.88 > 0.8

Watch me teach it here:

PRO TIP An error students make when comparing decimals is not lining up the decimal. I call this "pack and stack"!

Connect It!

"We have to compare decimals in our jobs, when running errands and playing sports, and in many other places in our lives! Let's discover some situations where you might have to compare decimals in everyday life."

- Example 1 – Buying Snacks: You want to buy a bag of chips that costs $1.49, and you have $1.35. Do you have enough money to buy it?
- Example 2 – Measuring Height: You go to an amusement park with height requirements. You are 4.55 feet tall, and the rules say you must be at least 4.25 feet tall to ride. Are you tall enough?
- Example 3 – Running a Race: You ran a sprint in 9.56 seconds today, and your personal record is 9.43 seconds. Did you beat your record today?

    Team Talk: "Discuss places where you've seen decimals being compared." Have students share, and don't forget to add their responses to your anchor chart!

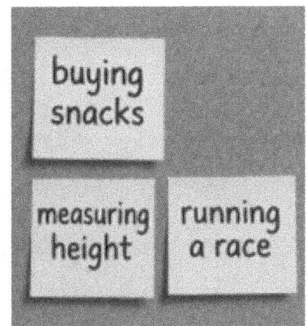

Hands-On Activity: Price Check Challenge!

Duration: 10–15 minutes

Materials

- Grocery ads, toy catalogs, or access to a website like Amazon
- Recording sheet with number lines
- Poster board and markers

Intro

You've been given some money to go shopping and can buy 5–10 items from the catalog/website. You want your money to stretch as far as it can, so you're going to compare decimals to make sure you're getting the best deals possible.

Activity Steps

1. Students choose two similar items (e.g., a bike from 2 different brands/companies) or items in the same category (i.e., two different video games) and record both on their recording sheet. "Make sure to pack and stack and line up place values!"

2. Students use decimal place value to compare and order the prices by creating number lines, charts, or visual models to show their comparisons.

3. Repeat with 5–10 items or as time allows.

4. Students create a "Best Deals" flyer or poster for the store and explain their reasoning for which items are the best value.

5. Students present their flyers to the class and explain how they used decimals to make smart shopping choices.

   - Enrichment: Budget Challenge: Give students a budget (e.g., $50) and ask them to "shop" for the most items without going over.

Guided Practice

1. Compare 0.36 and 0.4 using place value.

   Step 1: Line up the decimals by the decimal point: 0.36 and 0.40.
   Step 2: Compare from left to right. Tenths: 3 vs. 4. Since 4 is greater, 0.36 < 0.4.

2. Plot and compare 0.72 and 0.68 on a number line.

   Step 1: Draw a number line from 0 to 1, marking tenths and hundredths.
   Step 2: Locate 0.72 between 0.7 and 0.8, and 0.68 between 0.6 and 0.7. Since 0.72 is
   farther right, 0.72 > 0.68.

3. Determine if 2.15 = 2.150.

   Step 1: Recognize that adding a zero at the end does not change the value.
   Step 2: Compare place values. They match exactly, so 2.15 = 2.150.

Practice Questions

Name/Date _____

Fill in the Blanks

1. When comparing 0.89 and 0.9, line them up as 0.89 and _____. Then
   0.89 < 0.90 because the tenths digits are 8 vs. _____.

2. On a number line, 0.45 is to the _____ of 0.4 because the hundredths
   make it greater by 0.05.

3. The symbol for "0.207 is less than 0.21" is written as 0.207 _____ 0.21.

Multiple Choice

1. Which comparison is correct for 3.07 and 3.1?

   A. 3.07 > 3.1

   B. 3.07 = 3.1

   C. 3.07 < 3.1

   D. None of the above

2. How does 0.6 compare to 0.59?

   A. 0.6 < 0.59 because 59 hundredths is more than 60 hundredths

   B. 0.6 > 0.59 because 6 tenths equals 60 hundredths

   C. They are equal

   D. Cannot compare without a number line

3. The point at 0.3 on a number line compares to 0.25 as

   A. 0.3 = 0.25

   B. 0.3 > 0.25

   C. 0.3 < 0.25

   D. 0.3 is not plottable

Short Answer

1. Explain why 0.8 > 0.79 using place value.

_____

_____

_____

2. Order these decimals from least to greatest: 1.2, 1.02, 1.20. Justify your answer using symbols.

_____

_____

_____

3. How does plotting on a number line help compare 0.45 and 0.5?

_____

_____

_____

Open Response

You are timing a sprint with finishes of 12.34 seconds and 12.4 seconds. Compare them using <, >, or =. Plot both numbers on a number line, and use place values to explain why one is greater. Then add a third time, 12.37 seconds, and order all three from least to greatest.

Exit Ticket

1. Compare 5.67 and 5.6 using place value. Write the correct symbol and explain why the hundredths digit matters.

_____

_____

_____

2. Plot 0.82 and 0.80 on a number line. Which is greater, and how many hundredths apart are they? (Use the space below to draw your number line.)

MEASUREMENT & DATA

Measurement

Notes from the Classroom

I was coaching 8th grade cheer during a heated basketball game against a rival school. The opposing team's coach's behavior was out of control! He was running out to the court, screaming at kids, calling kids out, etc. Eventually, he was thrown out of the game, but right before that happened, one of my sassy cheerleaders put her poms down, threw her hands in the air, and yelled, "Dude, this is 8th GRADE BASKETBALL, NOT THE OLYMPICS!"

Sometimes, kids do know best :)

–Wendy Guidry

Section 1: Converting Measurement Units

In this section we will explore how to convert between different units of measurement. Students will learn how to switch between larger and smaller units in both metric and customary systems, such as how to convert millimeters to meters or inches to feet. They will also apply these conversions to solve concrete problems involving length, weight, volume, time, and money. Measurement songs, like Numberock's "Metric Units" song, will guide students through memorable examples, showing how the same patterns apply to meters, grams, and liters.

Learning Goals

I can (students will) identify relative sizes of measurement units within metric and customary systems; convert from larger to smaller units or from smaller to larger units using tables or operations; solve word problems involving distance, time, volume, mass, and money by applying these conversions.

Teacher Tip

Begin with hands-on exploration by having students measure classroom objects with rulers, scales, and measuring cups in both metric and customary units. This helps them build intuition about relative sizes before moving into conversions. Use visual aids such as conversion charts or mnemonic devices like "King Henry Died By Drinking Chocolate Milk" to make metric prefixes easier to remember. Real-world activities, such as working with recipes, also strengthen understanding. Finally, have students build their own conversion tables step-by-step, reinforcing that when converting from a larger unit to a smaller unit, we multiply, and when converting from a smaller unit to a larger unit, we divide.

Whole Brain Learning

As the song describes a millimeter, have students pinch their fingers close together to show something tiny. For centimeters, they can point to their fingernail or snap side to side. For meters, students stretch their arms wide or strum an air guitar. For kilometers, they march around the room as if walking along the shore. During the chorus, when the song repeats conversions such as "10 millimeters = 1 centimeter," have students clap or jump on each number. These movements make the conversion patterns memorable.

Lesson: Converting Units of Measurement

Duration: 25-30 minutes (break up each unit of measurement by day)

Intro

Students will convert measurements within the same system (e.g., inches to feet, minutes to hours) and solve real-world problems using these conversions.

VIP Vocabulary

- Convert: To change from one unit to another
- Unit: A standard amount used to measure something (like inches, feet, minutes)
- Length: How long something is (e.g., inches, feet, yards)
- Capacity: How much something can hold (e.g., cups, pints, gallons)
- Weight: How heavy something is (e.g., ounces, pounds)
- Units of Time: Measuring how long something takes (e.g., seconds, minutes, hours)
- Customary System:
  - Length: inch, foot, yard, mile
  - Weight: ounce, pound, ton
  - Capacity: cup, pint, quart, gallon
  - Time: second, minute, hour
- Metric System:
  - Length: millimeter, centimeter, meter, kilometer
  - Mass: gram, kilogram
  - Capacity: milliliter, liter
  - Time: second, minute, hour

Systems of Measurement

- Say: "Units help us measure things like length, weight, liquid volume, and time. Sometimes we measure things in different ways. You might say your pencil is 12 inches long, but you could also say it's 1 foot long. That's called **converting**—changing from one unit to another. You'll learn how to do that using math and how to solve problems like the following:

🕐 "How many minutes are in 3 hours?"

📏 "How many inches are in 5 feet?"

🧃 "How many cups are in 2 quarts?"

   "You'll become a measurement expert and use what you learn in cooking, sports, travel, and more!"

Metric Measurements

Let's Rock!

Now's a great time to play Numberock's "Metric System" song!
NUMBEROCK Metric System Song | 3rd Grade–4th Grade Measurement

Metric System	
https://numberock.com/mttm/	

Questions Before, During, and After the Song

Before: "What do you think a millimeter looks like compared to a meter? Can you find something in the classroom that is about a centimeter long?"

During: Pause at 1:34, when the song says "10 millimeters = 1 centimeter." Ask: "How many millimeters are in 2 centimeters? Why do you think the song uses the same pattern for grams and liters?"

After: The song says a 10-minute walk on the shore is about a kilometer. Ask: "How would you explain to a friend that 1 kilometer equals 1,000 meters using examples such as soccer fields? Pair up and share your explanations."

Customary Measurements

Length

Let's Rock!

Now's a great time to play Numberock's "Inches, Feet, & Yards" song!

Inches, Feet, & Yards	
https://numberock.com/mttm/	

Questions Before, During, and After the Song

Before: "How do inches, feet, and yards relate to one another? Can you guess how many inches fit in one foot?"

During: "Pause at 0:26: "12 inches inside 1 foot." What is similar or different about counting by 12s in the customary system compared to counting by 10s in the metric system?"

After: "The song says: "Put them three times as far and make a yard." Pair up and demonstrate how 3 feet make 1 yard, then have students work together with their partners to try and figure out how many inches are in a yard."

Weight

Questions Before, During, and After the Song

Before: Why might it be helpful to convert between smaller and larger units (e.g., ounces to pounds, or pounds to tons)?

During: Pause around 0:46: Try solving a similar problem (e.g., "If a treasure chest weighs 4 tons, how many pounds is that?"). What about converting tons back into pounds or ounces?

After: In your own words, explain how you convert from ounces → pounds → tons.

Consider two objects: one is 640 ounces, another is 18 pounds. Which weighs more? Convert to the same unit to compare.

Capacity

Questions Before, During, and After the Song

Before: "What does "capacity" mean? When we talk about how much liquid something can hold, what are some units you already know (cups, gallons, pints, etc.)?"

During: "Pause around 0:54 *when it shows cups → pints*"

"If 2 cups = 1 pint, how many cups would be in 3 pints? Could you compute that? What operation do you use to convert cups to pints?"

After: "Explain in your own words how many cups are in a quart or gallon?

Why does it matter to know conversions? When might you use this knowledge?"

Time

Let's Rock!

Now's a great time to play Numberock's "Units of Time" song!

Units of Time Song | Months of the Year Rap Video by NUMBEROCK

Units of Time	
https://numberock.com/mttm/	

Questions Before, During, and After the Song

Before: What units of time do you already know (seconds, minutes, hours, days, weeks, months, etc.)?

During: Pause around 2:29: 10 years is a decade, 100 years is a century, 1,000 years is a millennium. What pattern do you see in the names and sizes?"

After: List all the units of time mentioned in the video, from smallest to largest (seconds, minutes, hours, days, weeks, months, years, decade, century, millennium). How does knowing these units help you in everyday life (e.g., planning time, understanding calendars or thinking about history)?

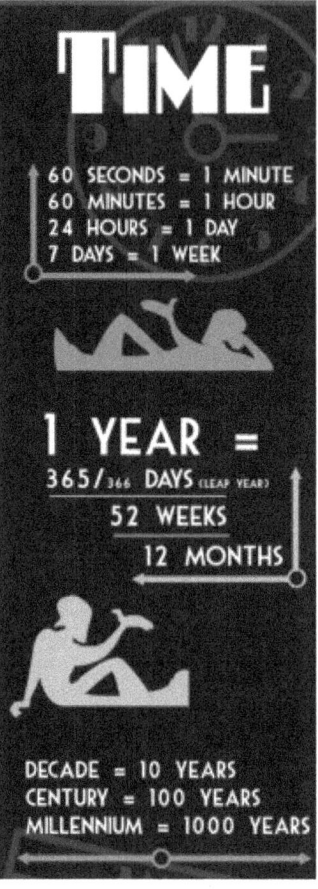

How to Convert Units of Measurement

- Say: "When converting ANY units of measurement, first identify whether you are going from a BIGGER unit to a smaller unit or from a smaller unit to a BIGGER unit. From BIG to small, we multiply. From small to BIG, we divide."

Watch me teach it here:

PRO TIP Use the hand motions to remember which operation to use!

- Ask: "If you ran 36 inches, how many feet did you run? What do you know that could help you figure that out?"
- Do: Draw a table and use the anchor chart to locate the information needed to solve.

Feet	Inches
1	12
2	24
?	36

- Say: "In this problem, we're going from inches (what we know) to feet (what we're trying to solve for). This is a small to BIG problem, so we divide. If 12 inches is in 1 foot, 36 inches would equal 3 feet because 36/12 = 3."

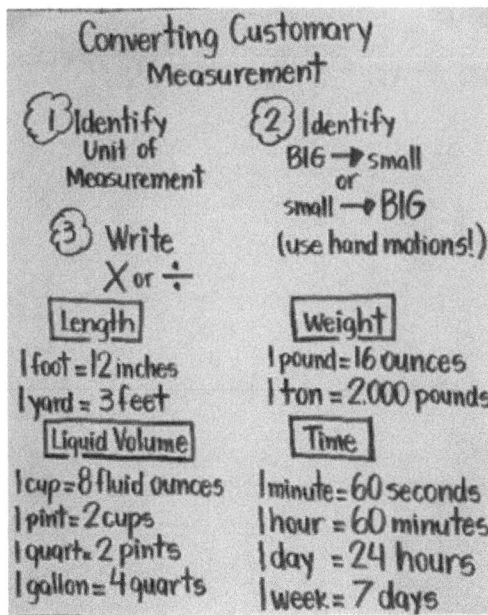

Let's Practice!

- Ask: "If a recipe calls for 2 quarts of milk, but you have only containers that measure one cup at a time, how can you figure out how many to use? Do we use multiplication or division to solve?"
- Do: Have students assist in creating a table to help solve!

Quarts	Cups
1	4
2	8
3	12

- Say: "The second row tells us the solution to this question! We are going from quarts (what we know) to cups (what we're trying to solve for). This is a BIG to small problem, so we multiply. If 1 quart is 4 cups, 2 quarts is 8 cups because 2 x 4 = 8."

Connect It!

"Measurements sometimes have to be converted into different units—why do you think that is?"

- Example 1 – Cooking: Converting cups to quarts or teaspoons to tablespoons
- Example 2 – Travel: Changing miles to feet or minutes to hours
- Other examples:
- Sports: Measuring track length in meters or yards
- Shopping: Comparing ounces and pounds on food labels
- School schedules: Figuring out how many minutes are in a class period

Team Talk: "Discuss situations where you've had to convert units of measurement."
Have students share, and don't forget to add their responses to your anchor chart!

Hands-On Activity: Gallon Man Saves the Party!

Duration: 10–15 minutes

Materials

- Construction paper
- Markers, colored pencils, or crayons
- Black pen or pencils for labeling
- Index cards or notebook paper for writing conversions

Intro
"You're planning a party and serving delicious drinks but you're not sure what containers are available to serve it in! Convert between gallons, quarts, pints, and cups to make sure you have your bases covered!"

Activity Steps

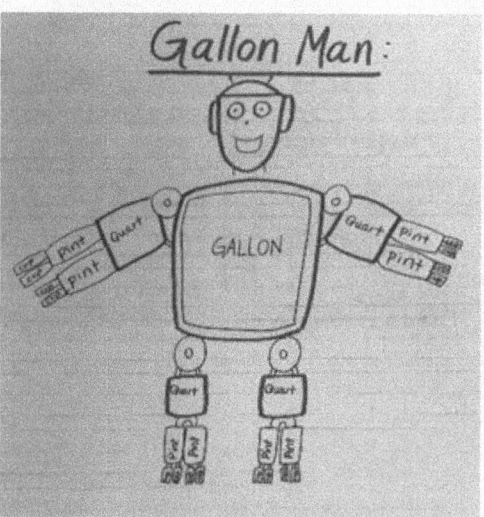

1. Build Your Gallon Man

- Use construction paper to create a Gallon Man with
  - 1 gallon body
  - 4 quart arms/legs
  - 8 pint hands/feet
  - 16 cup fingers/toes
- Label each part clearly.

2. Party Planning Challenge
Students work in teams to plan a party for 20 guests. They must:

- Choose drinks (lemonade, juice, etc.).
- Decide how much of each drink is needed (e.g., 20 cups of lemonade).
- Convert this measurement between gallons, quarts, pints, and cups using Gallon Man.

3. Trade and Grade

- Swap conversions with another team and have them check your work while you check theirs!

Enrichment:

- Create a digital version of Gallon Man using drawing tools.
- Write a story or comic about Gallon Man helping someone at a grocery store.
- Design a poster or infographic showing conversions.

Guided Practice

1. Convert 5 meters to centimeters.

   Step 1: Recall the conversion. 1 meter = 100 centimeters.
   Step 2: Multiply to convert to smaller units. 5 × 100 = 500.
   Step 3: Record in a table: meters | centimeters → 5 | 500.

2. Solve: If a recipe calls for 2 liters of water, how many milliliters is that?

   Step 1: Recall that 1 liter = 1,000 milliliters.
   Step 2: Multiply to convert to smaller units. 2 × 1,000 = 2,000 ml.
   Step 3: Check with a benchmark: A small water bottle is about 500 ml, so four bottles
           equal 2 liters.

3. A park path is 3 kilometers long. How many meters is that, and if you walk it in 30 minutes,
   what is the time per kilometer?

   Step 1: Convert distance. 1 kilometer = 1,000 meters, so 3 kilometers = 3 × 1,000 meters
           = 3,000 meters.
   Step 2: Divide to find rate. 30 minutes ÷ 3 kilometers = 10 minutes per kilometer.
   Step 3: Show on a number line from 0 to 3 km with equivalent meters labeled.

Practice Questions

Name/Date _____

Fill in the Blanks

1. There are _____ inches in 4 feet.

2. Convert 2,500 meters to kilometers: _____ kilometers.

3. A bottle holds 1,500 milliliters. That is the same as _____ liters.

Multiple Choice

1. How many ounces are in 2 pounds

   A. 20   C. 4,000

   B. 32   D. 2

2. If 1 kilometer = 1,000 meters, how would you convert 5,000 meters to kilometers?

   A. Multiply by 1,000

   B. Divide by 1,000

   C. Add 1,000

   D. Subtract 1,000

3. The song compares a meter to a guitar length. Which is the best estimate for a
   door's height?

   A. 2 millimeters

   B. 2 centimeters

   C. 2 meters

   D. 2 kilometers

Short Answer

1. Explain why you multiply when converting from pints to cups but divide when converting from cups to pints.

   _____

   _____

   _____

2. Convert 4 kilometers to meters and describe a real-world example such as running

   _____

   _____

   _____

3. If a bag weighs 3,000 grams, how many kilograms is that? How does this connect to the song's pattern for liters?

   _____

   _____

   _____

Open Response

You are planning a 2 kilometer hike. Convert this to meters. If it takes 20 minutes to hike 500 meters, how long will the entire hike take? Solve step-by-step and show your reasoning with a number line. (Use the space on the bottom of the page to draw your number line.)

Exit Ticket

1. Convert 27 feet to yards. Explain how this matches Inches, Feet, Yards song's "one yard just won't be complete if it does not contain 3 feet."

   _____

   _____

   _____

2. A juice box is 250 milliliters. How many would fill 1 liter? Show your work.

   _____

   _____

   _____

Notes from the Classroom

I once had a student have the most amazing A-HA moment. Educators live for the a-ha's, the clicks, the magical moment of a new understanding. The conversation went something like this: "Ohhhhhhh. Mrs. Furr, I get it now! <sweet little precious tilts her head and proceeds to tenderly rub the side of my face>. "That's why you're called Mrs. Furr. You have a lot of fur on your face!" <sweet little precious has wide eyes and a very proud smile for finally understanding>. "Mmmm . . . what an umm . . . interesting connection you have made there. Actually baby, Mrs. Furr took the last name of her husband, and that is . . . nevermind. Go sit down, love."

–Brittany Morgan Furr

Section 2: Perimeter and Area of Rectangles

In this section we will learn about the perimeter and the area of rectangles. Perimeter measures the distance around a shape, while area measures the space inside it. We will use simple formulas to calculate both and apply them to real-world situations, such as finding how much fencing is needed for a garden or how much carpet is needed for a room. Numberock's "Perimeter and Area" song shows these ideas through a cafeteria example with chairs and tables, helping students see how perimeter measures the distance around a shape, while area measures the space inside it.

Learning Goals

I can (students will) solve problems involving the perimeter and area of rectangles using formulas. They will apply these skills to real-world situations with whole-number side lengths, including problems with unknown sides.

Teacher Tip

Begin the lesson by playing the "Perimeter and Area" song. Before playing it, teach the following chant, so students can familiar with the concept: "Chairs around the edge, tables in the space, perimeter's the outline, area fills the place." This chant helps students remember the difference between perimeter and area before they work with formulas.

Whole Brain Learning

Have students act out perimeter and area as they listen to the song. One student stands in the center as a table (area), while others stand around as chairs (perimeter). As the song adds tables in a row, students link arms to extend the rectangle and add more chairs.

Lesson: Perimeter and Area

Duration: 20–25 minutes

Intro

Perimeter and area can be easily confused, so it's important to expose students to lots of real-world and hands-on examples of finding each and seeing how they relate to each other. This is a great unit to get outside of the classroom and explore.

> # VIP Vocabulary
>
> - Perimeter: The distance around a shape
> - Area: The amount of space inside a shape
> - Length: How long something is
> - Width: How wide something is
> - Unit Square: A square with a side length of 1 unit, used to measure area

Finding Perimeter and Area

> ### Let's Rock!
>
> Now's a great time to play Numberock's "Area and Perimeter" song!
>
> | Area and Perimeter | |
> |---|---|
> | https://numberock.com/mttm/ | |
>
> **Questions Before, During, and After the Song**
>
> Before: "What do you already know about the names of the outside edge and the inside space of a rectangle? How could counting chairs and tables help you understand these ideas?"
>
> During: Pause at 0:56, when the song says, "that's the perimeter." Ask: "What is the difference between counting the chairs around the tables and counting the tables themselves?"
>
> After: At 1:50 the perimeter increased to eight for three tables. Why did the number of chairs (perimeter) increase by two each time a table was added, and how did that relate to area?
>
>

PRO TIP PeRIMiter has the word RIM in it! Remember that it means the outside of something! When we find the area, we count the SQUARES! This reminds students that the unit for area is always in square units.

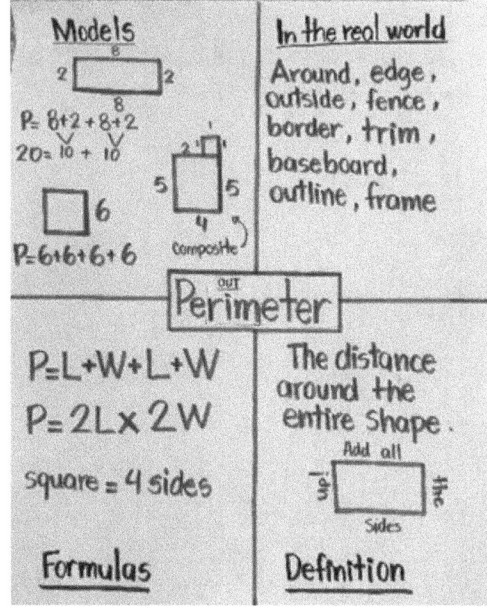

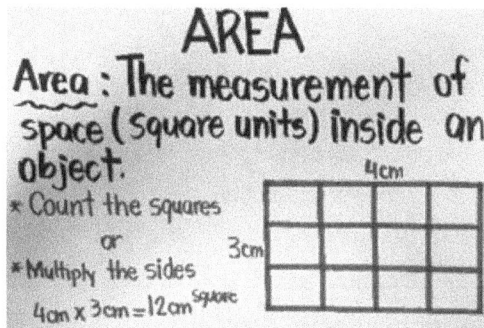

Watch me teach it here:

- Say: "Imagine you're designing a garden for our school. You need to know how much fencing to buy and how much grass seed to spread. What is the difference between these two measurements? How do they relate to each other?"
- Do: Draw a model of the garden on the board. Have students use their background knowledge to label area and perimeter and discuss how you find each.
- Ask: "Which of the following are measuring perimeter?"
  - Walking around a basketball court
  - Painting the walls of my room
  - Putting a border on my bulletin board
  - Laying carpet in my bedroom
- Say: "First, we're going to learn how to find the perimeter of rectangles and squares and use the perimeter to find missing side lengths. Remember, perimeter is like walking around the edge of a shape – it's the distance around the ENTIRE shape." Use hand motions here!

Relationship Between Area and Perimeter

- Say: "Try to make a rectangle with a perimeter of 24 units. How many different rectangles can you find?"
- Do: Have students share their models on the board and find the area of each rectangle or square as a class.
- Ask: "What happens to the area of each rectangle as you change the length and width? What observations can you make about the relationship between the perimeter and the area of your rectangle?"

Let's Practice: 1- and 2-Step Problems

1. **Area Mystery**

   A rectangle has a **width of 4 units** and an **area of 32 square units**.

   ☞ What is the missing **length**?

2. **Perimeter Puzzle**

   A rectangle has a **length of 7 units** and a **perimeter of 24 units**.

   ☞ What is the missing width?

3. **Double Trouble**

   A rectangle has an **area of 45 square units** and a **perimeter of 28 units**.

   ☞ What are the length and width of the rectangle?

4. **Shape Sleuth**

   A rectangle has a **perimeter of 30 units**. One side is **5 units**.

   ☞ What is the AREA of the rectangle?

5. **Design Challenge**

   You are designing a garden that is **6 units wide** and needs to have a **perimeter of 54 units**.

   ☞ How long should it be?

Connect It!

"Finding area and perimeter go hand in hand—let's explore some real-world examples!"

Example 1: Designing a Garden

- Perimeter: You need to know how much fencing to buy to go around the garden.
- Area: You need to know how much soil or mulch you need in order to cover the inside of the garden.

Example 2: Framing a Picture

- Perimeter: Determines the length of the frame material needed
- Area: Tells how much space the picture takes up

Other examples:

Sports: Building a court, field, or pool

   Home renovation or building: Painting walls and borders, laying tile, carpet, baseboards, wallpaper, etc.

   Team Talk: "Discuss situations where you've had to find area and perimeter." Have students share, and don't forget to add their responses to your anchor chart!

Hands-On Activity: Design Your Dream Park

Duration: 10–15 minutes

• Show the students examples of real parks and discuss how space is used.

Materials

• Blank paper for sketching
• Grid paper
• Ruler
• Pencils
• Materials for creating a 3D model of the park (optional)
• Technology to present the park (PowerPoint, Canva, etc. – optional)

Intro

"The city is building a new park and needs your help designing it. You'll need to plan areas for fun, relaxation, and nature – all using rectangles!"

Activity Steps

1. Planning the Park

"You are given 10,000 square feet of open land to create a park on. Using your planning sheet, sketch a rough layout and label each section and decide on dimensions for each (e.g., 20 × 15 for a playground). Park elements can include the following:

• playground
• picnic area
• community garden
• sports field
• walking path
• dog park
• splash pad
• restroom facility
• seating area
• butterfly garden"

2. Calculate Area & Perimeter

Use rulers and grid paper to draw each section to scale, and calculate the following:

• Area = length × width
• Perimeter = 2 × (length + width)

3. Design

Create a neat, labeled blueprint of your park on grid paper. Each section should be color-coded and labeled with the following:

- Name of the section
- Dimensions
- Area and perimeter

4. Gallery Walk

Display students' work around the room and take a gallery walk to enjoy!

Enrichment:

- Budget It: Assign a cost per square unit and have students find the cost of each element and the total cost of the park.
- 3D Model: Build a model of the park using cardboard or paper.

Guided Practice

1. Find the perimeter and area of a rectangle that is 5 units long and 3 units wide.

   Step 1: Recall the formulas: Perimeter = 2 × (length + width). Area = length × width.

   Step 2: Plug in the numbers: Perimeter = 2 × (5 + 3) = 16 units. Area = 5 × 3 = 15 square units.

2. A garden has a perimeter of 24 feet and a length of 8 feet. What is the width, and what is the area?

   Step 1: The perimeter of the garden is 24 feet. A rectangle has two lengths and two widths.

   Step 2: Since there are two pairs of equal sides, divide 24 by 2. 24 ÷ 2 = 12, so the length + width = 12.

   Step 3: The length is 8 feet, so we subtract 8 from 12 to find the width. 12 - 8 = 4 feet.

   Step 4: Now find the area. Area = length × width, so 8 × 4 = 32 square feet.

3. A room needs 36 square meters of flooring and is 9 meters long. What is the width, and what is the perimeter?

   Step 1: Use the area formula: 36 = 9 × width, so width = 4 meters.

   Step 2: Calculate the perimeter: 2 × (9 + 4) = 26 meters.

Practice Questions

Name/Date _____

Fill in the Blanks

1. The perimeter of a rectangle with length of 7 units and a width of 2 units is _____, and the area is _____.

2. If the area of a rectangle is 20 square units and the length is 5 units, the width is _____ units.

3. A rectangle has a perimeter of 18 units. If the width is 4 units, the length is _____ units.

Multiple Choice

1. What is the perimeter of a rectangle that is 6 units long and 4 units wide?

   A. 10 units

   B. 20 units

   C. 24 units

   D. 12 units

2. A park has an area of 48 square feet and a width of 6 feet. What is the length?

   A. 8 feet

   B. 12 feet

   C. 6 feet

   D. 54 feet

3. If a rectangle's perimeter is 30 units and its area is 54 square units, which could be its dimensions?

   A. 3 by 18

   B. 6 by 9

   C. 5 by 10

   D. 4 by 12

Short Answer

1. Explain the difference between the perimeter and the area of a rectangle using the chairs and tables example from the song.

   _____

   _____

   _____

2. A fence around a yard is 28 meters long. If the yard is 10 meters wide, what is the length, and what is the area?

   _____

   _____

   _____

3. A rectangle has a length of 6 feet and a width of 4 feet. If the length is doubled and the width stays the same, what happens to the perimeter? What happens to the area?

   _____

   _____

   _____

Open Response

Imagine you are designing a rectangular playground with a perimeter of 40 meters. Choose whole-number dimensions and calculate the area. Then choose a different set of whole-number dimensions with a perimeter of 40 meters. Which rectangle has the larger area?

_____

_____

_____

_____

_____

Exit Ticket

1. Draw a rectangle with whole-number sides, label the perimeter and area, and explain why the perimeter is twice the sum of the length and the width.

2. A rectangle has an area of 24 square units. List two different possible pairs of whole-number dimensions. Then find the perimeter of each rectangle.

   _____

   _____

   _____

Notes from the Classroom

Anyone else get interrupted during their job today having to address the exclamation, "Uh! Why is there meat in your shoe!?" When investigating, i.e., turning rapidly and giving annoyed teacher eye to the exclaimer, asking, "What are you saying over here?" you are met with, "Sorry Miss, for real he got chopped up meat in his shoe!" Said shoe meat smuggler responds with, "It's not just like slabs of meat in the shoe I'm wearing, it's ham in this little plastic container thing. I was carrying too much stuff after lunch and it kept falling off my Chromebook, so I figured I could carry it in my gym shoe." I continued discussing rational numbers, despite this irrational conversation!

–Cristy E Christensen

Section 3: Representing Data with Line Plots

In this section we will explore the world of line plots, where measurements with fractions turn into visual stories that show patterns in data. We will learn how to create line plots using fractions such as halves, quarters, and eighths; plot data points accurately; and solve problems by adding or subtracting fractions from the information shown. Numberock's "Line Plot" song takes us through examples like growth data and comparing the heights of students in different grades, showing how line plots represent real-world measurements and help us analyze data.

Learning Goals

I can (students will) collect and represent data with fractional values on a line plot, and use common denominators to write equivalent fractions and solve problems involving addition and subtraction of fractions using data.

Teacher Tip

Begin by collecting real student data, such as how much each student grew in inches during the past year. To build confidence, start with whole-number data before moving to fractions. Then play the song to reinforce the steps of finding common denominators and plotting data points. Encourage the class to sing the chorus together to memorize the process.

Whole Brain Learning

Have students act out building a line plot with their bodies during the chorus. As the song describes recording data above a number line, students stretch their arms wide. They then jump forward in small steps as they chant "plot what you've got on the line plot."

Lesson: Line Plots

Duration: 15–20 minutes

Intro

In fourth grade, students move to plotting fractions on a line plot in addition to whole numbers!

VIP Vocabulary

- Line Plot: A graph that shows frequency of data along a number line
- Data: Information collected for analysis
- Measurement: The size, length, or amount of something
- Frequency: How often a value appears
- X: A symbol used to mark data points on a line plot
- Median: The middle value in a set of ordered data
- Mode: The value that appears most often in a data set
- Range: The difference between the greatest and least values in a data set

---

Making Line Plots

Let's Rock!

Now's a great time to play Numberock's "Line Plots with Fractions" song!
"Line Plots with Fractions" Song

Line Plots with Fractions	
https://numberock.com/mttm/	

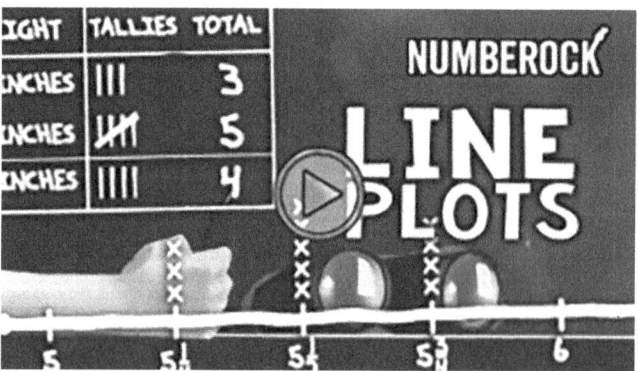

LINE PLOTS

Line Plots Display Data Points Above a Number Line To Show How Frequently Values Occur.

How Many Inches 5th Graders Grew?

Stacks of Xs shows the number of times the same data point occurs

Always title your graph and label the unit

Each X represents the amount one student grew in a year

Inches

A Fifth Grade Class Collected Data About Their Growth To Find Out How Many Inches They Grew In A Year. Their Teacher Displayed That Data On a Line Plot To Show How Frequently Each Data Point (or, each student's growth occured.

Questions Before, During, and After the Song

Before: "What do you think a line plot looks like? How could it help us show measurements such as how much we have grown in fractions of an inch?"

During: Pause at the chorus: "First, find a common denominator." Ask: "Why do we need a common denominator when working with fractional data on a line plot?"

After: "In the bridge, the song compares fourth and fifth graders' growth. How would you use the line plots to add up total growth for each grade and subtract to find the difference? Pair up and share your explanation."

- Say: "Today, we'll measure data and use a line plot to show what we found. Line plots help us see patterns and answer questions about the data we collect."
- Ask: "What kinds of things can we measure in real life? Why might someone want to organize their data? What do you notice when you look at a line plot?"
- Do: Draw a large open number line on the board. Hand out rulers to students and have them measure their pencil to the nearest 1/4 inch (review fractions on a number line from Chapter 4 if needed!) and record their measurement on a sticky note.
- Ask: "What is the smallest measurement we have? What is the largest? How do those measurements help us determine how to set up the number line?"
- Do: Discuss and draw intervals on the number line using the sticky notes. Plot each measurement on the number line with an "x" to represent each value.

Analyze the plot:

- "Which length is most common?"
- "Are there any outliers?"
- "What's the total number of items measured?"
- "What is the difference between the longest and shortest measurement?"
- "How does the line plot help you understand the data better than you would if you just looked at a list?"

Finding Median, Mode, and Range

Median, Mode, Range

Median: the number in the <u>middle</u>. (don't forget to put them in order first!)

4, 6, 6, 7, [11], 12, 13, 16, 18

Range: the difference between the largest and the smallest number.

[4], 6, 6, 7, 11, 12, 13, 16, [18]

18 - 4 = [14]

Mode: the number that <u>appears</u> the <u>most</u>. (not the greatest number)

4, [6], [6], 7, 11, 12, 13, 16, 18

Intro

Fourth graders use line plots to help them solve questions about the data, including finding the median, mode, and range.

- Say: "Let's look at the questions we just answered about our data set. Now we'll use math vocabulary to represent some of the common problems we solved."
- Say: Instead of saying "the most common," we can find the **MODE**. The **MODE** is the number or numbers in a data set that occur the **MOST** often. Be careful not to confuse **MOST** with HIGHEST! The mode might not be the largest number. It's also possible to have no mode if no numbers occur more than once!
- Ask: "What is the mode of the data set above?"
- Say: "It's important to put our data in order from least to greatest so we can make observations about the set as a whole. When we look at the number in the middle of the data set, that's called finding the **MEDIAN**. Just like a median in a road is in the middle of the road, the median of a data set splits the data down the middle. If there is more than one **MEDIAN**, we add them together and divide that by 2."
- Ask: "What is the median of the data set above?"
- Say: "Earlier, we answered a question about the difference between the longest and shortest measurements. That's called the **RANGE**. You might have heard that word used in "vocal range" or "driving range." It just means how far something spans from start to finish! We subtract the lowest measurement from the highest to find the **RANGE**."
- Ask: "What was the range of our earlier data set? How could you use this information to make a decision (e.g., which pencil size to order for the class)?"

Connect It!

"When we organize data on line plots, it's so helpful in making inferences and observations about our lives! How can it help us set goals?"

Example 1: Math Fluency Practice

- Scenario: Students time themselves solving math facts.
  - Mode: Most common time
  - Median: A good benchmark
  - Range: Shows improvement in speed and consistency

- Goal Setting: "I want my median time to be under 2 minutes."

Example 2: Reading Minutes Logged in a Week

- Scenario: Students track how many minutes they read each night.
  - Mode: Most common reading time
  - Median: Middle value of reading times
  - Range: Shows the spread of reading habits

- Why It Matters: Helps students reflect on their reading routines and set goals

Other examples:

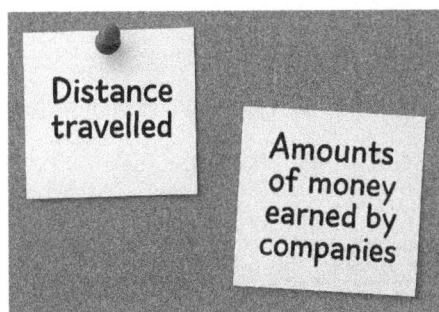

- Sports: goal setting and fitness tracking
- Math: fluency practice
- Class activities: fundraising goals

Team Talk: "When have you used data to help you understand something important in your life?" Have students share, and don't forget to add their responses to your anchor chart!

Hands-On Activity: Water Bottle Data Detectives

Duration: 10–15 minutes

Materials

- Rulers or measuring tapes
- Water bottles (metal, glass, or plastic)
- Sticky notes or data cards
- Chart paper or whiteboard for line plot
- Markers

Intro

"Our school is thinking about giving every student a reusable water bottle. But they want to know what size would be best. Your job is to collect data and help make that decision."

Activity Steps

1. Measure the length of the water bottles and record the measurement on a sticky note.
2. Add the data to a class line plot.
3. Students work in pairs or small groups to calculate mode, median, and range.
4. Discuss findings as a class.

   Reflection Questions:
   - "Based on our data, what water bottle size should we choose?"
   - "How did the line plot help us make a decision?"
   - "What would happen if we had more data?"
5. Students vote or write a short recommendation based on the data.

Guided Practice

1. Create a line plot for the following data on pet lengths in inches: 1 1/2, 1 1/4, 1 3/4, 1 1/2, 2.

    Step 1: Find a common denominator of 4 and convert: 1 2/4, 1 1/4, 1 3/4, 1 2/4, 2.
    Step 2: Draw a number line from 1 to 2 inches with 1/4-inch intervals.
    Step 3: Plot the points, label the axis "Inches," and title the line plot "Pet Lengths."

2. Use this daily rainfall data in inches: 3/4, 1/2, 1, 3/4, 1/4. Make a line plot and find how much more rain fell on the day with the highest rainfall than on the day with the lowest rainfall.

    Step 1: Convert to fourths: 3/4, 2/4, 4/4, 3/4, 1/4.
    Step 2: Draw a number line from 0 to 1 with quarter intervals and plot the points.
    Step 3: Subtract lowest from highest: 4/4 − 1/4 = 3/4 inch more.

3. Create a line plot to display the following fruit weights in pounds: 1/8, 3/8, 1/4, 1/2, 3/8. Then find the total weight of the two fruits with the most common weight.

    Step 1: Convert to eighths: 1/8, 3/8, 2/8, 4/8, 3/8.
    Step 2: Draw a number line from 0 to 1/2 and mark it in eighths.
    Step 3: The most common weight is 3/8 (it appears twice). Add 3/8 + 3/8 = 6/8 or 3/4 pound.

Practice Questions

Name/Date _____

Fill in the Blanks

1. On a line plot with quarter-inch intervals, the data point at 1/2 is equivalent to _____ fourths.

2. If a line plot shows growth data of 1/2, 3/4, 1, and 1/2, the total combined growth is _____ inches.

3. A line plot must include a _____ on the bottom for units and a title at the _____.

Multiple Choice

1. In a line plot of fractional data, why do we find a common denominator?

    A. To make the numbers whole

    B. To plot equivalent fractions accurately

    C. To subtract whole numbers only

    D. To skip intervals

2. A line plot shows four data points at 1/4 and two data points at 1/2. What is the difference between the total of the 1/2 values and the total of the 1/4 values?

    A. 1/4   C. 0

    B. 1/2   D. 1

3. A line plot shows one data point at 3/8 pound and one data point at 1/2 pound. How much greater is 1/2 than 3/8?

    A. 1/3   C. 1/5

    B. 1/8   D. 1/10

Short Answer

1. Explain how to convert 1/2 and 1/4 to fractions with like denominators for plotting on a line plot with quarter-inch intervals.

_____

_____

_____

2. Create a line plot for the following data: 2/8, 4/8, 6/8, 2/8. What fraction of the data points is the most frequent value?

3. Why must the number line be divided into eighths when plotting data such as 3/8? What could happen if you used fourths instead?

_____

_____

_____

Open Response

A survey shows the following daily reading times of five students (in hours): 1 1/4, 1 1/2, 3/4, 1, and 1 1/4. Create a line plot. How much more total time did the two students who read 1 1/4 hours spend reading than the student who read 3/4 of an hour?

Exit Ticket

1. Draw a line plot for this data: 1/4, 1/2, 3/4, 1/2. Explain how you divided the number line.

2. Find the total of all the data on your line plot.

_____

_____

_____

Notes from the Classroom

I was teaching geometry and going over vocabulary so I sent home a parent letter so they could see what we were learning in the classroom. A parent contacted me wondering why I was teaching a *Star Trek* term. He thought vertex was vortex and was very confused!

–Linda Darlington

Section 4: Understanding Angles

In this section we are going to explore the world of angles, which are formed when two rays meet at a common endpoint called a vertex. We will learn to classify angles as acute, right, obtuse, or straight, and then use a protractor to measure angles accurately. The "Angles" song will guide us through these ideas with fun rhymes and real-world examples, like pizza slices or moose antlers, helping us clearly understand how to identify, measure, and work with angles.

Learning Goals

I can (students will) recognize angles as shapes formed by two rays that share an endpoint called a vertex. I can classify angles as acute, right, or obtuse, measure angles in whole-number degrees using a protractor, and find the measure of an unknown angle by adding or subtracting known angle measures.

Teacher Tip

Begin with an angle hunt around the classroom. Have students look for right angles in door corners or windows, acute angles in clock hands, and obtuse angles in furniture edges. After building familiarity with angle types, introduce the protractor as a tool to measure what they have found. Using hands or arms to form angle "rays" makes this lesson especially engaging, and estimating those angles connects students' bodies to the abstract concepts.

Whole Brain Learning

As the song plays, have students use their arms to act out the angles described. For acute angles, bring arms close together like a narrow V. For right angles, form an L shape. For obtuse angles, spread arms wide like moose antlers.

Lesson: Understanding Angles

Duration: 15–20 minutes

Intro

Students will understand angles as geometric shapes formed by two rays with a common endpoint, measure angles in degrees, and classify angles as acute, right, obtuse, or straight.

VIP Vocabulary

- Angle: A figure formed by two rays sharing a common endpoint
- Vertex: The point where two rays meet to form an angle
- Ray: A line that starts at one point and goes on forever in one direction
- Degree: A unit used to measure angles
- Protractor: A tool used to measure angles
- Acute Angle: Less than 90°
- Right Angle: Exactly 90°
- Obtuse Angle: Greater than 90° but less than 180°
- Straight Angle: Exactly 180°

Angle Types

Intro

An angle is made when two rays meet at a point called the vertex. We measure how "open" the angle is in degrees. A full circle is 360°, so angles are just parts of that circle.

Let's Rock!

Now's a great time to play Numberock's "Angles" song!

Types of Angles Song | Acute, Obtuse & Right Angles Video | 4th Grade

Angles
https://numberock.com/mttm/

Questions Before, During, and After the Song

Before: "What kinds of angles do you think you see in everyday objects, like a slice of pizza or the corner of a book? If you put two small angles together, what kind of angle might they form?"

During: Pause at 0:51, when the song says, "Between 90 and 180, an angle is obtuse."

Ask: "Why do you think an obtuse angle is described as wider than acute or right angles?"

After: Replay the bridge of the song on protractors starting around 1:11. "How would you explain to a friend the steps to line up the rays and count the degrees?" Have students pair up: one demonstrates with a real protractor while the other explains their partner's steps back to the class.

Acute Angles

- Say: "An acute angle is small and cute—like the tip of a slice of pizza or the corner of a triangle."
- Do: Draw an acute angle on the board. Have students make acute angles with their arms or pencils and then sketch one in their notebooks.
- Ask: "Can you find something in the room that makes a small, sharp angle? Why do you think it's called 'acute'?"

Between **ZERO** and **NINETY**
An angle is acute.
This angle's **SMALL** and skinny
And kind of cute.

Right Angles

- Say: "A right angle looks like the corner of a piece of paper or a book. It's a perfect square corner, one that measures 90°."
- Do: Draw a right angle and label it 90°. Use a corner of a paper to find right angles around the room. Have students make acute angles with their arms or pencils and then sketch one in their notebooks.
- Ask: "What objects around you have right angles? Why do you think right angles are important in building things?"

Obtuse Angles

- Say: "An obtuse angle is wide and open – like when you lean back in your chair!"
- Do: Draw an obtuse angle on the board. Have students make obtuse angles with their arms or pencils and then sketch one in their notebooks. Ask them to estimate its size.
- Ask: "How can you know from just looking at it that an angle is obtuse? What happens if you continue opening the angle until it becomes straight?"

Straight Angles

- Say: "A straight angle is a straight line. It looks like a flat road or a ruler."
- Do: Draw a straight angle and label it 180°. Have students use their arms to model one.
- Ask: "What's the difference between a straight angle and a line?"

Measuring Angles

Intro

A protractor helps us measure how open an angle is. We measure in degrees, just like a thermometer measures temperature.

- Ask: "Why do you think we need to measure angles? What would happen if we built something with the wrong angle?"
- Do: Draw an acute, right, obtuse, and straight angle on the board. Model how to line up the protractor:
  - Place the midpoint on the vertex.
  - Line up one ray with the 0° line.
  - Read where the other ray points.

Practice Together: Measure 2–3 angles as a class. Ask students to estimate first, then measure.

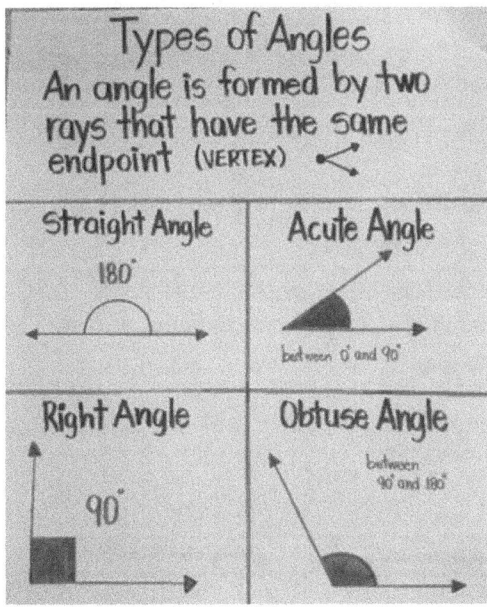

Watch me teach it here:

PRO TIP The best way to practice understanding and to attain mastery is by using hand motions for each angle. Imagining your head is the vertex, and use the positions above to represent each angle.

Connect It!

"Angles are everywhere! From the corners of picture frames to the hands of a clock, angles help us understand turns, directions, and design."

Example 1 – Construction & Architecture: Measuring angles is essential when we're designing buildings, roofs, stairs, and door frames.

- A carpenter uses a protractor or angle finder to ensure corners are exactly 90° (right angles) or to create sloped roofs with obtuse angles.

Example 2 – Navigation & Maps: Pilots, sailors, and hikers use angles to determine direction and turns.

- A compass uses degrees to show direction (e.g., turning 45° northeast or 90° east).

Other examples:

- Clock Reading: At 3:00, the hands form a right angle (90°); at 6:00, they form a straight angle (180°).
- Sports: Coaches and athletes use angles to improve performance (a basketball player adjusts the angle of their shot for better accuracy; a gymnast uses body angles to perfect form).
- Drivers turn the steering wheel at specific angles to make turns. A sharp turn might be close to 90°, while a gentle curve might be 45°.

Team Talk: "Where have you seen someone use a tool to measure an angle? Can you think of a time when measuring an angle helped solve a problem?" Have students share, and don't forget to add their responses to your anchor chart!

Hands-On Activity: Go on an angle hunt!

Duration: 10–20 minutes

Materials

- Notebook or clipboard and paper
- Pencil
- Protractor (or use estimation)

Intro

"You're headed on an angle hunt! Angles are everywhere in the real world. Let's head outside (or take a journey around our classroom) and see how many you can find!"

Activity Steps

1. Head outside or explore the classroom to find as many angle types as possible in 10 minutes.

2. Students draw the real-world example and the angle measurement (with a protractor or by estimation) and then share and discuss.

Tips: Incorporate technology by allowing students to take pictures of the angles they find!

Guided Practice

1. Classify an angle of 120°.

    Step 1: Recall the ranges: acute is less than 90°, right is 90°, and obtuse is greater than 90° but less than 180°.

    Step 2: Since 120° is more than 90° but less than 180°, it is an obtuse angle.

2. Measure the angle formed by two rays that look like the hands of a clock at 3:00.

    Step 1: Place the protractor's center hole at the vertex where the rays meet.

    Step 2: Align one ray with the zero mark on the protractor.

    Step 3: Count up along the scale to where the other ray points. The measure is 90°, which is a right angle.

3. A 150° angle is made up of a 90° angle and another angle. What is the measure of the missing angle?

    Step 1: The total angle is 150°. One part is 90°.

    Step 2: Subtract to find the missing part: 150° − 90° = 60°.

    Step 3: The missing angle measures 60°, which is an acute angle.

Practice Questions

Name/Date _____

Fill in the Blanks

1. An angle measuring exactly 90 degrees is called a _____ angle.

2. To measure an angle, place the _____ hole of the protractor at the vertex and align one ray with zero.

3. An angle that measures 180 degrees is called a _____ angle.

Multiple Choice

1. Which type of angle measures greater than 90, but less than 180 degrees?

    A. Acute   **C.** Right

    B. Obtuse   **D.** Straight

2. If one ray is at 0° on your protractor and the other is at 145°, what type of angle is it?

    A. Right   **C.** Acute

    B. Obtuse   **D.** Straight

3. If an angle of 120° is split into two equal parts, what is the measure of each part?

    A. 60°   **C.** 240°

    B. 90°   **D.** 30°

Short Answer

1. Explain the difference between an acute angle and an obtuse angle, giving an example of each.

    _____

    _____

    _____

2. Sketch a 135° angle by first drawing a 90° angle and then adding another 45°.

3. How many degrees are in a straight angle? A straight angle is made up of a 45° angle and a 135° angle. Show how you know these two angles form a straight angle.

_____

_____

_____

Open Response

Imagine you have a pizza cut into slices forming angles of 30°, 90°, and two slices forming angles of 120°. Classify each angle, explain how their measures add up to a full circle of 360°. Then write a short story about sharing the pizza, explaining how the size of the angle affects the size of the slice.

_____

_____

_____

_____

_____

Exit Ticket

1. Classify a 75° angle and explain how you would draw it with a protractor.

_____

_____

_____

2. A whole angle measures 160°. One part measures 70°. What is the measure of the other part? Then classify both angles as acute, right, or obtuse.

_____

_____

_____

Unit 5

GEOMETRY

08 Classifying Shapes

Notes from the Classroom

I used to teach pre-k, so I taught every subject. We had a science center with little observation containers. During our insect and bugs study, I had various deceased critters in those containers. One morning, I replaced one of our dead flies with a dead spider, you know, to add variety. One of my little fellas comes running up to me and says "Ms. Wilcox! One of our flies turned into a spider!" I had to gently explain what I had done. It was such a cute and innocent moment.

–Cari Wilcox Henegar

Section 1: Identifying and Classifying Two-Dimensional Figures

In this section we are going to explore the world of two-dimensional figures by identifying their sides, vertices, and angles. We will then use these features to classify figures like triangles and quadrilaterals. Along the way, we will discover how to recognize parallel and perpendicular lines, measure and estimate angles, and understand that the angles inside quadrilaterals always add up to 360 degrees. The "Quadrilaterals" song will guide us with a campfire sing-along as we learn the properties of trapezoids, parallelograms, rectangles, rhombuses, and squares.

Learning Goals

I can (students will) identify and draw points, lines, rays, and angles; classify two-dimensional figures based on properties such as parallel and perpendicular lines and right angles; and measure and estimate angles in whole-number degrees.

Teacher Tip

Bring geometry into the real world by showing students familiar objects: a pizza box for rectangles, a diamond shape for a rhombus, or railroad tracks for parallel lines. Before playing the song, give students cut-out shapes and have them sort them into groups based on properties such as "has right angles" or "has parallel sides." This concrete-to-abstract approach prepares students to see connections during the video.

Whole Brain Teaching

During the song, invite students to act out the shapes. For parallelograms, lean your forearms in tandem to show two sets of parallel lines. For trapezoids, slant forearms apart to show one pair of lines is not parallel. For rectangles, form an L shape with elbows. For rhombuses, stretch arms into a diamond. For squares, make a box in front of your chest by placing both hands in toward the opposite elbow. When the song reminds us that quadrilaterals have angle sums of 360 degrees, have students spin in a full circle to embody the idea of a complete rotation.

Lesson: Identifying and Classifying Two-Dimensional Figures

Duration: 15–20 minutes

Intro

Students will identify and classify two-dimensional figures based on their attributes (sides, angles, symmetry) and understand how shapes relate to one another in a hierarchy.

VIP Vocabulary

- Polygon: A closed figure with straight sides
- Quadrilateral: A polygon with 4 sides
- Triangle: A polygon with 3 sides
- Parallel Lines: Lines that never cross and that stay the same distance apart
- Perpendicular Lines: Lines that meet to form right angles
- Right Angle: An angle that measures 90°

Polygons

Say: "A polygon is a closed shape made of straight lines. It can be identified and named by the number of sides and angles it has. Let's explore how we can sort and describe these shapes."

Let's Rock!

Now's a great time to play Numberock's "Polygons" song!

Polygons	
https://numberock.com/mttm/	

Polygons Song

Questions Before, During, and After the Song

Before: What do you already know about polygons? Define a polygon in your own words (closed shape, straight sides, vertices).

During: Pause around 0:43: What does the prefix *tri-* or *quad-* tell you? How many sides/vertices do those shapes have? Can you find real-world examples like in the video?

After: Think about all the shapes throughout the video. What is one thing they all have in common?

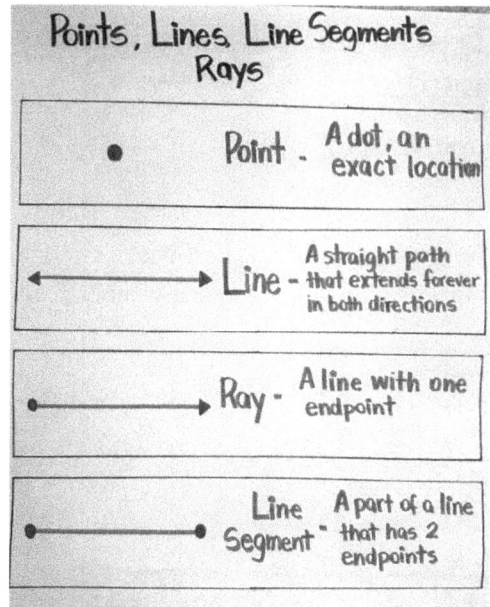

Ask: "What makes a shape a polygon? What vocabulary do we need to be able to describe polygons?"

Do: Draw a polygon on the board. Discuss the parts of the polygon and label.

Watch me teach it here:

PRO TIP Use hand motions to demonstrate each of the vocabulary words so it sticks! When it's time to dismiss, tell students to "line segment" up!!

Types of Lines

Say: "Lines can be straight, cross each other, or meet at perfect angles. Let's learn how to spot and name them."

Let's Rock!

Now's a great time to play Numberock's "Types of Lines" song!

Types of Lines Song: Parallel, Perpendicular & Intersecting Lines

Types of Lines	
https://numberock.com/mttm/	

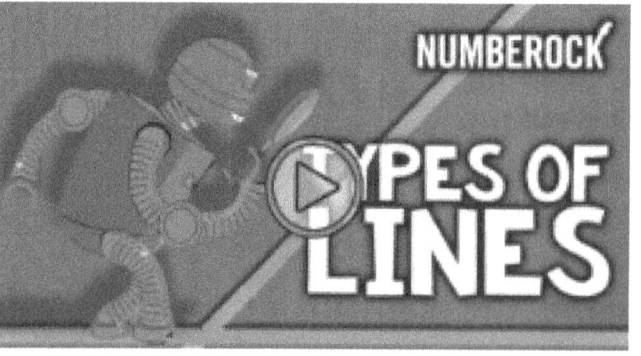

Questions Before, During, and After the Song

Before: What do you already know about parallel, perpendicular, and intersecting lines?

During: Pause at 1:46: What does perpendicular mean? How are perpendicular lines different from parallel lines?

After: Define or explain each type of line: parallel, perpendicular, intersecting. Give an example of each type of line (drawing or real-world). How are perpendicular lines related to intersecting lines?

Do:

- Show examples of **parallel**, **perpendicular**, and **intersecting lines**.
- Tell students to draw and label each type in their notebooks.
- Go on a line hunt in the classroom and label types of lines.

PRO TIP Use those robot arms every time the word perpendicular, intersecting, or parallel is said in class. As a quick exit ticket, say the vocabulary word at the door as students are walking out to lunch and have them flash the corresponding hand motion!

Watch me teach it here:

Angles

Say: "Angles can be open slightly, make the corner of a square, or open wide. Let's learn how to spot and name them."

Let's Rock!

Now's a great time to play Numberock's "Types of Angles" song!

Types of Angles Song | Acute, Obtuse & Right Angles Video

Types of Angles	
https://numberock.com/mttm/	

Questions Before, During, and After the Song

Before: What is an angle? What is an angle made up of (two rays or line segments and a vertex)?

During: Pause around 0:45: What makes a right angle special? What does it look like (e.g., like an L shape or corner of a square)? How can you know an angle is exactly 90°? What clues can you use visually or with tools (like a protractor) to make sure it's 90°?

After: If you add an acute angle and a right angle, is the sum always obtuse? Why or why not? Give an example with actual measures.

Do:

- Show examples of **acute**, **right**, and **obtuse angles**.
- Tell students to draw and label each type in their notebooks.
- Go on an angle hunt in the classroom and label types of lines.

Watch me teach it here:

PRO TIP Try not to giggle during big caboose! Hand motions are critical to locking it in!

Classifying Shapes

Quadrilaterals

Let's Rock!

Now's a great time to play Numberock's "Quadrilaterals" song!

Quadrilaterals	
https://numberock.com/mttm/	

Questions Before, During, and After the Song

Before: "What makes a square different from a trapezoid? Can you name something in our classroom that shows parallel lines?"

During: Pause at 0:21, at the lyrics "Trapezoids only have one set at a time." Ask: "How does a trapezoid look different from a parallelogram?"

After: The chorus of the song says all quadrilaterals have interior angles that add up to 360 degrees. Ask: "Why do you think that is true for every quadrilateral, no matter its shape? Pair up and explain, and then share your partner's idea with the class."

Do: Create an anchor chart for 2D shapes. Fill in the defining attributes as a class.

Ask:

- "What do you notice about the sides of a square?"
- "Can a rectangle and a square be part of the same shape family?"
- "What kind of lines do you see in a triangle?"

Do: Write the following attributes on index cards:

- 3 sides
- 4 sides
- 5 or more sides

- Right angle: exactly 90°
- Acute angle: less than 90°
- Obtuse angle: greater than 90°
- Parallel lines
- Perpendicular lines

Use the index cards to sort shapes on the anchor chart into groups that share common attributes.

Connect It!

"Shapes are everywhere! Understanding shapes helps us describe and create the world around us."

- Example 1: Architects use them to design buildings.
- Example 2: Artists use them in patterns.
- Example 3: Engineers use them to build strong structures.

Team Talk: "Discuss places where you've seen shapes being used." Have students share, and don't forget to add their responses to your anchor chart!

Hands-On Activity: Geometry Town: Design Your Own City!

Duration: 10–15 minutes

Materials

- Paper
- Pencils
- Optional: rulers or colored pencils

Intro

"You've been hired as a city planner! Your job is to design a town using geometric concepts like lines, angles, and shapes." Show a quick example (drawn on the board or projected): a simple town map with labeled geometric features.

Activity Steps

- Step 1: Student Task
  - In pairs or small groups, students sketch a **map of their town** on paper.
  - They must include and label the following:
    - At least 2 parallel streets
    - 1 perpendicular intersection
    - 1 park shaped like a quadrilateral
    - Buildings with different types of angles (acute, right, obtuse)
    - A river or path represented by a ray or line segment
- Step 2: Gallery Walk
  - Groups do a **1-minute gallery walk** or quick share-out.
  - Ask: "What geometric features did you use? How did they help organize your town?"

Guided Practice

1. Identify and classify a rectangle based on its properties.

   Step 1: Draw a rectangle and label its four sides. Notice that opposite sides are equal and parallel.

   Step 2: Mark the four right angles where the sides meet.

   Step 3: Classify it as a quadrilateral with two pairs of parallel sides and four right angles. Explain why it also fits under parallelograms.

2. Identify and classify a rhombus based on its properties.

   Step 1: Draw a rhombus and label that all four sides are equal in length and that opposite sides are parallel.

   Step 2: Mark the angles where the sides meet to show that opposite angles are equal.

   Step 3: Classify it as a quadrilateral with four equal sides and two pairs of parallel sides.

3. Identify a quadrilateral based on its properties.

   Step 1: Think of a quadrilateral that has two pairs of parallel sides and four right angles.

   Step 2: Use these properties to narrow down the possibilities and eliminate shapes that do not fit.

   Step 3: Identify the shape as a square or a rectangle and explain how its properties confirm this.

Practice Questions

Name/Date _____

Fill in the Blanks

1. A shape with exactly one pair of parallel sides is called a _____.

2. An angle that measures more than 90 degrees but less than 180 degrees is _____.

3. The sum of the interior angles in any quadrilateral is _____ degrees.

Multiple Choice

1. Which shape always has four right angles and two pairs of parallel sides?

   A. Trapezoid

   B. Rhombus

   C. Rectangle

   D. Triangle

2. Which quadrilateral can have exactly one right angle?

   A. Parallelogram

   B. Square

   C. Trapezoid

   D. Rhombus

3. You measure an angle as 45 degrees. What type of angle is it, and how does it compare to a right angle?

   A. Acute; smaller than 90 degrees

   B. Obtuse; larger than 90 degrees

   C. Right; equal to 90 degrees

   D. Straight; equal to 180 degrees

Short Answer

1. Explain how to identify parallel lines in a parallelogram and why it is different from a trapezoid.

_____

_____

_____

2. Explain why a rectangle and a rhombus are both special types of parallelograms.

_____

_____

_____

3. Explain how a square can be both a rectangle and a rhombus.

_____

_____

_____

Open Response

A quadrilateral has two pairs of parallel sides and four right angles. What shape could it be? Explain how you know by describing its properties, and name at least one other category this shape belongs to and explain why.

_____

_____

_____

_____

_____

Exit Ticket

1. Draw a square and label its properties: number of parallel sides, angle types, and total interior angle sum. Explain why it is also a rectangle. (Use the space to the left to draw your square.)

_____

_____

_____

2. Classify this description: a quadrilateral with four equal sides but no right angles. What shape is it, and how do you know?

_____

_____

_____

Notes from the Classroom

As an art teacher who loves incorporating math into my lessons, I would do a formal balance/symmetry lesson in February with all my grades, using hearts . . . soo many hearts! Students would make their work then create the tiniest hearts. I would sprinkle them over the kids saying "I'm showering you with love!" After experiencing this for a couple of years, one of my students says, "Oh good! It's Math-in-Tine Time!" and this project was forever renamed!

–Aurora Maynard

Section 2: Symmetry and Patterns

In this section we're going to explore the fascinating world of symmetry, where shapes can be divided by lines that create perfect mirror images on both sides! We'll learn how to recognize and draw lines of symmetry, identify which shapes are symmetric, and see how this concept appears everywhere in nature, art, and design. The "Symmetry Land" song will take us on a thrilling adventure through an amusement park filled with rides and shapes that show symmetry in action. From Ferris wheels and roller coaster loops to cracker squares and octagons, we'll discover how symmetry makes the world both beautiful and balanced.

Learning Goals

I can (students will) recognize a line of symmetry in a two-dimensional figure as a line that divides the figure into matching parts that are mirror images, identify symmetric figures, and draw lines of symmetry on various shapes.

Teacher Tip

Begin the lesson with three engaging activities that veteran teachers find especially effective for teaching symmetry.

First, use paper-folding exercises. Have students cut out shapes and fold them to discover lines of symmetry through hands-on exploration.

Second, introduce mirror-drawing, where students complete the missing half of a picture to see symmetry in reflection.

Third, send them on a symmetry hunt around the classroom or playground, searching for examples in doors, windows, artwork, and even their own faces.

After these warm-ups, play Numberock's "Symmetry Land" song, teaching your students the catchy chorus line before it begins: "Everywhere we look, we see lines of symmetry!" This sets a joyful tone and primes them to spot symmetry throughout the video.

Whole Brain Teaching

Turn "Symmetry Land" into a full-body experience. As the song plays, have students use movement to represent each example described. When the Ferris wheel appears, they can spin slowly with arms extended to show infinite lines through the center. During the pirate ship ride, have them sway side to side with one arm up like a mast, showing the vertical line of symmetry when their body is centered in between sways. When the cracker square appears, students can draw imaginary lines across the air for each fold, and when the octagon is mentioned, they can do the same for the 8 lines of symmetry shown in the video.

Lesson: Symmetry

Duration: 15–20 minutes

Intro

Students will identify and draw lines of symmetry in two-dimensional figures and recognize symmetrical patterns in the real world.

VIP Vocabulary

- Symmetrical: Able to be folded into two matching parts
- Line of Symmetry: The line that divides a shape into two equal, mirror-image halves

---

Say: "Symmetry is all about balance. If you fold a shape and both sides match perfectly, it has **symmetry**! The line where you fold it is called the **line of symmetry**."

Let's Rock!

Now's a great time to play Numberock's "Symmetry" song!
NUMBEROCK's Lines of Symmetry Video

Symmetry	
https://numberock.com/mttm/	

Questions Before, During, and After the Song

Before: "What do you already know about symmetry? Can you name a shape or object that looks the same on both sides if you fold it in half?"

During: Pause at 0:31, when the song says, "So each circle has infinity." Ask: "Why does the song say a circle has infinite lines of symmetry? How does that connect to the idea of mirror reflection?"

After: "The song mentions that a square cracker has four lines of symmetry and an octagon has eight. How would you explain to a friend why some shapes have more lines of symmetry than others?" Pair students up and have one explain while the other restates their partner's explanation to the class.

Do:

- Show a heart, square, triangle, and circle.
- Fold paper versions to find lines of symmetry.
- Draw the line of symmetry on the board for each shape.
- Use a mirror to show how one side reflects the other.

Ask: "Can you think of something in nature that looks the same on both sides? What happens if you fold a shape and the sides don't match? Can a shape have more than one line of symmetry?"

Connect It!

"Shapes and symmetry are everywhere! Understanding shapes helps us describe and create the world around us."

- Example 1: Nature: butterfly wings, leaves, snowflakes
- Example 2: Art & Design: logos, quilts, architecture
- Example 3: Everyday Objects: hearts, playing cards, road signs

Team Talk: "Discuss places where you've seen symmetry being used in the real world." Have students share, and don't forget to add their responses to your anchor chart!

Hands-On Activity: "Mirror Me!"

Duration: 5–10 minutes

Materials

- Tracing paper
- Drawing tools
- Mirror

Activity Steps

Step 1: Shape Investigation
- Choose a set of 2D shapes (e.g., square, rectangle, triangle, trapezoid, hexagon, circle).
- For each shape, draw it clearly and **identify all lines of symmetry**.
- To test symmetry, use a mirror or tracing paper, or fold the shape.

Step 2: Symmetry Sorting
- Sort the shapes into categories:
  - **No symmetry**
  - **One line of symmetry**
  - **Multiple lines of symmetry**
- Create a chart or poster showing your sorted shapes.

Step 3: Design a Symmetrical Scene
- Using only shapes with *at least one line of symmetry*, create a symmetrical picture or pattern.
- Your design must have **at least one line of reflectional symmetry**.

Step 4: Reflection
- Which shape had the most lines of symmetry? Why?
- How does symmetry help in design, architecture, or nature?

Enrichment:

- Symmetry Hunt: Find symmetrical shapes in your classroom or home.
- Create a Symmetry Book: Include drawings, symmetry lines, and explanations.
- Digital Exploration: Use online tools like Mathigon Polypad to explore symmetry interactively.

Guided Practice

1. Identify the lines of symmetry in a square.

   Step 1: Draw a square and imagine folding it so each side matches perfectly. Try folding vertically, horizontally, and diagonally.

   Step 2: Draw a line on each fold. Two lines go through the center (one vertical and one horizontal), and two go through opposite corners (diagonals).

   Answer: A square has four lines of symmetry.

2. Determine if a rectangle (that is not a square) has lines of symmetry and draw them.

   Step 1: Draw a rectangle and test folds vertically and horizontally through the midpoints; they should match, but the diagonals will not.

   Step 2: Draw the two lines of symmetry, one vertical and one horizontal.

   Answer: A rectangle has two lines of symmetry.

3. Check for symmetry in an equilateral triangle and draw any lines of symmetry.

   Step 1: Draw an equilateral triangle and fold from each vertex to the midpoint of the opposite side.

   Step 2: Each fold should create matching halves.

   Answer: An equilateral triangle has three lines of symmetry.

Practice Questions

Name/Date _____

Fill in the Blanks

1. A line of symmetry divides a shape into two _____ parts that are mirror images of each other.

2. A regular hexagon has _____ lines of symmetry, because this is how many ways you can fold it to create a perfect mirror reflection.

3. A rectangle has _____ lines of symmetry.

Multiple Choice

1. How many lines of symmetry does a circle have?

   A. 0   C. 4

   B. 1   D. Infinite

2. Which shape has exactly two lines of symmetry?

   A. Square

   B. Equilateral triangle

   C. Rectangle (not a square)

   D. Regular pentagon

3. In the "Symmetry Land" song, the roller coaster loop is described as having a line of symmetry. What does this mean?

   A. It can be divided into two matching halves

   B. It has four lines like a rectangle

   C. It has four lines like a square

   D. It has no symmetry

Short Answer

1. Explain why a heart shape has only one line of symmetry.

   _____

   _____

   _____

2. Name a shape with three lines of symmetry and describe where those lines are located.

   _____

   _____

   _____

3. A student says that a rectangle has four lines of symmetry. Do you agree or disagree? Explain your reasoning and describe where the lines of symmetry are located.

   _____

   _____

   _____

Open Response

Imagine you're preparing for a school event that needs a logo. Design a symmetrical logo, like a butterfly or flag. Look at the logo and mark at least one line of symmetry. Explain how you confirmed that the sides matched and describe why symmetry is important in design. (Use the space at the bottom of the page to draw your logo.)

_____

_____

_____

_____

_____

Exit Ticket

1. Draw a quick sketch of a shape with exactly one line of symmetry, and mark the line.

2. True or false: All rectangles have four lines of symmetry like squares. Explain why or why not.

   _____

   _____

   _____

Answer Key

Chapter 1: Place Value and Rounding

Section 1: Place Value of Whole Numbers
(4.NBT.1-2; BEST MA.4.NSO.1.1; TEKS 4.2B)

Fill in the Blanks

1. 10

2. 80,000 + 2,000 + 400

3. five

Multiple Choice

1. b) 10 times

2. b) 10 times

3. a) The 7 in the hundreds place is 10 times greater than the 7 in the tens place.

Short Answer

1. The 2 in 20,000 is ten times greater than the 2 in 2,000 because each move one place to the left increases the value by a factor of ten. The 2 in 20,000 represents 20,000, while the 2 in 2,000 represents 2,000.

2. Expanded form: 400,000 + 50,000 + 900.
   Word form: four hundred fifty thousand nine hundred.

3. There are 100 tens in 1,000 and 10 hundreds in 1,000.

Open Response

If Rob picks 6,000 blueberries and moves the 6 one place to the right to make 600, his new total is ten times less than the original amount. Example story: Rob had 6,000 blueberries in his basket, but he shared them evenly with 10 friends. Now each friend, including Rob, has 600 blueberries. The total 600 is ten times less than 6,000.

Exit Ticket

1. Expanded form: 70,000 + 8,000. The 7 is worth 10 times more than the 7 in 7,800 because moving one place to the left increases its value by a factor of ten, from 7,000 to 70,000.

2. 10 thousands make 10,000. One thousand equals 1,000. Ten thousands means $10 \times 1,000$ which equals 10,000. In the place-value system, multiplying by 10 moves the digit one place to the left.

Section 2: Comparing and Ordering Numbers
(4.NBT.2; BEST MA.4.NSO.1.3; TEKS 4.2C)

Fill in the Blanks

1. 40,000

2. <

3. greater (the larger number)

Multiple Choice

1. c) 321,654 > 312,654

2. c) greater than

3. b) 10 times

Short Answer

1. Both have 2 hundred-thousands, so we compare ten-thousands: 254,000 has 5 in the ten-thousands; 245,000 has 4 in the ten-thousands; since 5 > 4, 254,000 > 245,000.

2. 802,000; 812,000; 821,000

3. Both have 9 hundred thousands, so we compare the ten-thousands: 990,000 has 9 ten-thousands; 909,000 has 0 ten-thousands; because 9 ten-thousands > 0 ten-thousands, 990,000 > 909,000.

Open Response

Sample story: I'm a starving alligator staring at 30,000 fish on one side and 3,000 fish on the other. I chomp the 30,000 because it's greater – 30,000 has 3 ten-thousands (a 3 in the ten-thousands place) while 3,000 has zero ten-thousands. Since 30,000 is ten times as many as 3,000, my mouth points toward the bigger meal!

Exit Ticket

1. 42,000 > 24,000. The alligator faces 42,000 because it is greater (4 ten-thousands vs. 2 ten-thousands).

2. 560,000 appears further to the right because it is larger than 506,000 (same hundred-thousands digit 5, but 6 ten-thousands > 0 ten-thousands).

Section 3: Rounding Whole Numbers
(4.NBT.3; BEST MA.4.NSO.1.4; TEKS 4.2D)

Fill in the Blanks

1. 65,000

2. 850,000

3. 4,300,000

Multiple Choice

1. a) 840,000

2. c) 48,000

3. c) 100,000

Short Answer

1. 589,654 rounded to the nearest thousand is 590,000 because the hundreds digit is 6, which is 5 or greater, so the number in the thousands place rounds up from 9 to 10.

2. 9,876,543 rounded to the nearest million is 10,000,000 because the hundred-thousands digit is 8, which is 5 or greater, so the number in the millions place rounds up from 9 to 10.

3. 453,829 rounded to the nearest ten thousand is 450,000 because the thousands digit is 3, which is less than 5, so the number in the ten-thousands place stays the same.

Open Response

There are 23 + 28 + 32 = 83 students in total. When rounding each class to the nearest ten, 23 rounds to 20, 28 rounds to 30, and 32 rounds to 30. Adding those gives an estimate of 80 students. Rounding helps make quick estimates to plan things like food, chairs, and decorations without needing exact counts.

Exit Ticket

1. 3,465,321 rounded to the nearest ten thousand is 3,470,000 because the thousands digit is 5, which is 5 or greater, so the ten-thousands digit rounds up from 6 to 7.

2. Rounding is helpful when dealing with very large numbers because it makes them easier to read, compare, and estimate during calculations or planning.

Chapter 2: Computation with Whole Numbers

Section 1: Adding and Subtracting Whole Numbers (4.NBT.4; BEST MA.4.NSO.2.2; TEKS 4.4A)

Fill in the Blanks

1. 1,382

2. 438

3. regroup (or borrow)

Multiple Choice

1. b) Because two digits add to more than 9

2. d) Regroup from the hundreds place

3. c) Use subtraction (the inverse operation)

Short Answer

1. We need to regroup because some place-value sums are greater than 9. In the ones place, 6 + 9 = 15, so we write 5 ones and carry 1 ten to the tens place.

2. 1,204 − 867 = 337. You must regroup because 4 − 7 cannot be done. Since the tens place is 0, you borrow from the hundreds place. The hundreds become 1 hundred, the tens become 9 tens, and the ones become 14.

3. When subtracting 6,002 − 2,738, you must regroup across zeros. You borrow from the thousands place, turning the hundreds into 9 hundreds, the tens into 9 tens, and the ones into 12 ones before subtracting.

Open Response

287 + 428 = 715. First, line up the numbers by place value. Add the ones: 7 + 8 = 15, write down 5 and carry 1. Add the tens: 8 + 2 = 10, plus 1 = 11, write down 1 and carry 1. Add the hundreds: 2 + 4 + 1 = 7. The total number of chairs is 715. To check your work, use subtraction: 715 − 428 = 287, which proves the addition is correct.

Exit Ticket

1. 6,891 + 4,292 = 11,183. Yes, you need to regroup because 9 + 2 = 11 in the ones place, and adding 9 + 8 + 1 in the tens place also requires carrying.

2. 5,000 − 2,783 = 2,217. You borrow from the thousands place to make 10 hundreds, then regroup again to create enough tens and ones to subtract.

Section 2: Multiplying Whole Numbers (4.NBT.5; BEST MA.4.NSO.2.3; TEKS 4.4D)

Fill in the Blanks

1. place value

2. 120

3. add

Multiple Choice

1. B

2. B

3. B

Short Answer

1. Breaking numbers by place value (tens, ones, etc.) makes the multiplication simpler and clearer; you multiply smaller parts and then add them, reducing mistakes.

2. $12 \times 15 = (10 \times 15) + (2 \times 15) = 150 + 30 = 180$ carrots.

3. $28 \times 19 = (20 \times 19) + (8 \times 19) = 380 + 152 = 532$ cans.

Open Response

Each kid buys 23 trays, so 2 kids buy 46 trays. Each tray has 15 blueberries: $46 \times 15 = (46 \times 10) + (46 \times 5) = 460 + 230 = 690$ blueberries. Partial products help because you see how tens and fives contribute to the total before adding them.

Exit Ticket

1. $53 \times 6 = (50 \times 6) + (3 \times 6) = 300 + 18 = 318$.

2. Total bags = 32 + 25 = 57; $57 \times 8 = (50 \times 8) + (7 \times 8) = 400 + 56 = 456$ cans.

Section 3: Dividing Whole Numbers by One-Digit Divisors (4.NBT.6; BEST MA.4.NSO.2.4; TEKS 4.4F)

Fill in the Blanks

1. divisor; dividend

2. 90; 180

3. 0 (zero)

Multiple Choice

1. C

2. B

3. B

Short Answer

1. Both split the dividend into easy chunks of the divisor: the area model shows the chunks as rectangle sections (each width is a partial quotient), while partial quotients list and subtract those same chunks; the totals match.

2. $384 \div 8 = 48$ (e.g., $8 \times 40 = 320$; $384 - 320 = 64$; $8 \times 8 = 64$; $40 + 8 = 48$).

3. $252 \div 9 = 28$ (e.g., $9 \times 20 = 180$; $252 - 180 = 72$; $9 \times 8 = 72$; $20 + 8 = 28$).

Open Response

Sample answer: $624 \div 8$

Partial quotients: $8 \times 50 = 400 \rightarrow 624 - 400 = 224$; $8 \times 20 = 160 \rightarrow 224 - 160 = 64$; $8 \times 8 = 64 \rightarrow 64 - 64 = 0$; sum $= 50 + 20 + 8 = 78$.

Area model: Draw a rectangle of area 624, side 8; partition widths 50, 20, and 8 to make areas 400, 160, and 64; total width = 78.

Preference: (sample) I prefer partial quotients because I can flexibly choose large or small chunks and keep a clean running total.

Exit Ticket

1. $189 \div 9$: $9 \times 20 = 180 \rightarrow 189 - 180 = 9$; $9 \times 1 = 9 \rightarrow 9 - 9 = 0$; add partial quotients $20 + 1 = 21$.

2. It breaks division into understandable steps – repeated subtraction of known multiples – so you see how many groups you've taken and why the quotient makes sense.

Chapter 3: Understanding and Solving Problems

Section 1: Writing Equations and Expressions (4.OA.1-2; BEST MA.4.AR.2.1; TEKS 4.5A)

Fill in the Blanks

1. 15

2. 36

3. 10

Multiple Choice

1. C

2. C

3. C

Short Answer

1. 7 × 4 = 28. Max's brother has 28 apples.

2. 8 × 6 = 48. The 6 tickets cost $48.

3. 9 ÷ 3 = 3. Emma's friend has 3 stickers.

Open Response

Equation: 18 = 3 × J (where J represents Jacob's pencils). Divide 18 ÷ 3 = 6, so Jacob has 6 pencils. I divided because Lena's amount is 3 times Jacob's, so finding Jacob's means finding one of the three equal groups that make up 18.

Exit Ticket

1. 5 × 20 = 100. The school has 100 students.

2. 3 × 4 = 12. The watermelon weighs 12 pounds.

Section 2: Multistep Word Problems (4.OA.3; BEST MA.4.AR.1.1; TEKS 4.4H)

Fill in the Blanks

1. plan

2. divide

3. multistep

Multiple Choice

1. B

2. B

3. C

Short Answer

1. 44 + 80 = 124; 200 − 124 = 76 miles

2. 36 − 12 = 24; 24 ÷ 3 = 8 cookies each

3. 5 × 4 = 20; 20 − 6 = 14 markers

Open Response

Example problem: A class buys 6 boxes of pencils with 12 pencils in each box. They give 15 pencils to another class. How many pencils remain?

Solution: 6 × 12 = 72; 72 − 15 = 57 pencils. I multiplied first to find the total, then subtracted the amount given away.

Exit Ticket

1. 12 + 15 = 27; 40 − 27 = 13 miles

2. 3 × 6 = 18; 18 − 4 = 14 cars

Section 3: Factors and Multiples (4.OA.4; BEST MA.4.NSO.2.1; TEKS 4.4B)

Fill in the Blanks

1. prime

2. 2

3. 25

Multiple Choice

1. C

2. B

3. C

Short Answer

1. Examples: 12 (3 × 4), 15 (3 × 5).

2. 1 has exactly one factor (itself), not two distinct factors, so it is neither prime nor composite.

3. 5 rows and 5 columns (a 5 × 5 array).

Open Response (example for number 24)

Factor pairs: 1 × 24, 2 × 12, 3 × 8, 4 × 6 (arrays can show these).

First four multiples: 24, 48, 72, 96.

Classification: 24 is composite (more than two factors).

Real-world uses: You can arrange 24 chairs in rows and columns for different seating layouts (e.g., 3 × 8 or 4 × 6).

A gardener might plant 24 flowers in equal rows to fit a rectangular bed.

Exit Ticket

1. Factors of 32: 1, 2, 4, 8, 16, 32.

2. 54

Chapter 4: Fraction Concepts

Section 1: Equivalent Fractions (4.NF.1; BEST MA.4.FR.1.1; TEKS 4.3C)

Fill in the Blanks

1. equivalent

2. same

3. same

Multiple Choice

1. B
2. B
3. C

Short Answer

1. 4/12 ÷ 4/4 = 1/3. I divided both the numerator and denominator by their greatest common factor, 4.

2. 3/5 × 2/2 = 6/10 and 3/5 × 3/3 = 9/15.

3. You can't divide by 3 because 2 and 5 are not both divisible by 3. You can only divide by a number that is a common factor of both the numerator and denominator.

Open Response

4/8 and 1/2 are equivalent fractions, so they represent the same amount. Using a fraction bar, both fill exactly half of the bar. On a number line, 4/8 and 1/2 point to the same location – halfway between 0 and 1. So my friend and I ate the same amount of chocolate.

Exit Ticket

1. 3/4 × 2/2 = 6/8 and 3/4 × 3/3 = 9/12.

2. Multiplying by the same number keeps the fraction's value the same because you're multiplying by a form of one (e.g., 2/2 = 1), which doesn't change the value, only how it's expressed.

Section 2: Comparing Fractions (4.NF.2; BEST MA.4.FR.1.2; TEKS 4.3D)

Fill in the Blanks

1. less
2. denominator
3. greater

Multiple Choice

1. B) <
2. B) 3/5
3. A) 2/4

Short Answer

1. 3/5 is greater than 1/2 because 3 is more than half of 5. 3/7 is less than 1/2 because 3 is less than half of 7. So 3/5 > 3/7.

2. You can multiply or divide both the numerator and denominator of 1/2 by the same number. Since 1 × 4 = 4 and 2 × 4 = 8, 4/8 = 1/2, so they are equivalent.

3. Finding a common denominator lets you compare fractions with the same-sized parts. Once the denominators match, you can directly compare the numerators to see which is greater.

Open Response

Draw two rectangles of the same size. Shade 2 out of 3 equal parts in one rectangle and 2 out of 5 equal parts in the other. The rectangle with 2/3 shaded has more area covered, showing 2/3 is greater than 2/5. On a number line, 2/3 is also farther to the right than 2/5, confirming it's the larger fraction.

Exit Ticket

1. 5/6 > 5/8. The denominators show the size of each part; eighths are smaller than sixths, so 5/6 covers more of the whole.

2. 3/4 > 2/4. Both have the same denominator, and 3 is greater than 2, so 3/4 represents a larger portion of the whole.

Chapter 5: Operations with Fractions

Section 1: Adding and Subtracting Fractions with Like Denominators (4.NF.3; BEST MA.4.FR.2.1; TEKS 4.3E)

Fill in the Blanks

1. numerators

2. denominator

3. 5/6

Multiple Choice

1. B

2. C

3. A

Short Answer

1. 3/4 + 1/4 = 4/4 because the parts (fourths) are the same size, and 3 parts plus 1 part equals 4 parts, which makes one whole.

2. 2/8 + 3/8 = 5/8, because both fractions have the same denominator, and you only add the numerators. Total eaten: 5/8.

3. The denominator tells the size of each part; when parts are the same size, only the number of parts (the numerator) changes.

Open Response

Ben and Mia ate 1/6 + 4/6 = 5/6 of the pie. They did not finish it because 5/6 is one part less than a whole pie. Only if they had eaten 6/6 would the entire pie be gone.

Exit Ticket

1. 2/9

2. The denominator stays the same because the size of each fractional part doesn't change; you're just increasing or decreasing how many of those equal parts you have.

Section 2: Multiplying Fractions by Whole Numbers
(4.NF.4; BEST MA.4.FR.2.2; TEKS 4.3F)

Fill in the Blanks

1. whole number

2. denominator

3. 2

Multiple Choice

1. b) Multiply by the top, then divide by the bottom

2. a) 3/3

3. a) 2

Short Answer

1. Using repeated addition: 1/2 × 6 means adding 1/2 six times (½ + ½ + ½ + ½ + ½ + ½ = 3). Using the algorithm: multiply 6 × 1 = 6, then divide by 2, which also equals 3.

2. A visual model shows 3 × 1/2 as three groups of one – half. On a number line, start at 0 and make three jumps of 1/2 to land at 3/2 (1 1/2). In a pizza model, three halves combine to make one whole and one half.

3. The phrase "multiply by the top, divide by the bottom" simplifies the rule for multiplying a whole number by a fraction, reminding students to multiply the whole number by the numerator and then divide by the denominator to get the correct part of the whole.

Open Response

For 3 × 2/5, use a number line from 0 to 3 wholes, divided into fifths. Each group of 2/5 is two fifths of a whole. Three groups of 2/5 make 6/5, which equals 1 1/5. Using the algorithm: multiply 3 × 2 = 6, then divide 6 ÷ 5 = 6/5 = 1 1/5. Both methods show the same result.

Exit Ticket

1. 5 × 3/4 = 15 ÷ 4 = 3 3/4.

2. 2/3 of 9 = (9 × 2) ÷ 3 = 18 ÷ 3 = 6 miles.

Chapter 6: Decimals and Fractions

Section 1: Understanding Decimals and Fractions
(4.NF.5-6; BEST MA.4.FR.1.3; TEKS 4.2G)

Fill in the Blanks

1. 0.9

2. 25

3. 0.06; 60

Multiple Choice

1. b) 0.45
2. b) 70/100
3. c) 50/100

Short Answer

1. 0.8 is the same as 8/10 because the 8 is in the tenths place, meaning 8 parts out of 10 equal parts. On a number line from 0 to 1 divided into 10 equal parts, 0.8 is at the eighth mark.

2. 0.06 = 6/100 because the 6 is in the hundredths place. In money terms, this equals 6 cents out of one dollar.

3. 3/10 = 30/100. Comparing 30/100 and 25/100, 30/100 is larger because 30 hundredths is more than 25 hundredths.

Open Response

Eating 35 out of 100 slices is 35/100, which equals 0.35. Eating 3/10 of another pizza equals 30/100 or 0.30. Together, 35/100 + 30/100 = 65/100, which is 0.65 of a whole pizza.

Exit Ticket

1. 12/100 = 0.12 because the 1 is in the tenths place and the 2 is in the hundredths place, meaning 12 hundredths in total.

2. 4/100 = 0.04. For example, if a rope is 1 meter long, 0.04 meters equals 4 centimeters, showing that hundredths represent very small parts of a whole.

Section 2: Comparing Decimals
(4.NF.7; BEST MA.4.FR.1.4; TEKS 4.2H)

Fill in the Blanks

1. 0.09
2. right
3. <

Multiple Choice

1. c) 3.07 < 3.1
2. b) 0.6 > 0.59 because 6 tenths equals 60 hundredths
3. b) 0.3 > 0.25

Short Answer

1. 0.8 > 0.79 because 0.8 has 8 tenths (or 80 hundredths) while 0.79 has only 7 tenths and 9 hundredths (79 hundredths). 80 hundredths is greater than 79 hundredths.

2. 1.02 < 1.2 = 1.20. Both 1.2 and 1.20 are equal since the zero in the hundredths place doesn't change the value.

3. Plotting on a number line helps because you can see that 0.45 is slightly to the left of 0.5, meaning it's smaller by 0.05.

Open Response

12.34 < 12.4 because 12.4 equals 12.40; the tenths are the same, but the hundredths digit 3 is less than 4. On a number line, 12.34 is to the left of 12.4. When adding 12.37, the order from least to greatest is 12.34, 12.37, 12.4.

Exit Ticket

1. 5.67 > 5.6 because in 5.67, the hundredths digit (7) makes it greater than the hundredths digit in 5.60. The hundredths place helps show smaller differences between decimals.

2. 0.82 > 0.80. They are 0.02, or 2 hundredths, apart. On a number line, 0.82 is two marks to the right of 0.80.

Chapter 7: Measurement

Section 1: Converting Measurement Units
(4.MD.1–2; BEST MA.4.M.1.1; TEKS 4.8A)

Fill in the Blanks

1. 48

2. 2.5

3. 1.5

Multiple Choice

1. b) 32

2. b) Divide by 1,000

3. c) 2 meters

Short Answer

1. There are 2 cups in a pint, so to go from pints to cups you multiply by 2 (more, smaller units). To go from cups to pints you divide by 2 (fewer, larger units).

2. 4 km = 4,000 m. Example: a 4 km fun run.

3. 3,000 g = 3 kg because 1,000 g = 1 kg. This matches the liters pattern where 1,000 milliliters = 1 liter (thousands-to-one conversion).

Open Response

2 kilometers = 2000 meters. If 500 meters takes 20 minutes, then 2000 meters is four groups of 500 meters: 4 × 20 = 80 minutes total. On a number line, mark 0, 500, 1000, 1500, and 2000 meters; each jump of 500 meters represents 20 minutes, totaling 80 minutes.

1. 27 ÷ 3 = 9, so 27 feet = 9 yards. This matches the song because each yard contains 3 feet, so 27 feet makes 9 groups of 3 feet.

2. 1 liter = 1,000 milliliters; 1,000 ÷ 250 = 4. Answer: four.

Section 2: Perimeter and Area of Rectangles (4.MD.3; BEST MA.4.GR.2.1; TEKS 4.5D)

Fill in the Blanks

1. 18; 14

2. 4

3. 5

Multiple Choice

1. b) 20 units

2. a) 8 feet

3. b) 6 by 9

Short Answer

1. Perimeter measures the distance around a shape (like the edge of a table), while area measures the space inside it (like how many chairs fit around the table).

2. The fence (perimeter) is 28 meters, so 28 = 2 × (10 + L). Divide by 2: 14 = 10 + L, so L = 4 meters. The area is 10 × 4 = 40 square meters.

3. When the length is doubled, the perimeter increases but does not double because only one dimension changes. The area doubles because the length is multiplied by the same width, doubling the total space.

Open Response

If the playground's perimeter is 40 meters, one possible design is 10 meters long and 10 meters wide (10 + 10 + 10 + 10 = 40). The area is 10 × 10 = 100 square meters. If you change the shape to 12 meters long and 8 meters wide, the perimeter stays 40, but the area becomes 12 × 8 = 96 square meters, slightly smaller. The closer the sides are to equal, the greater the area for a fixed perimeter.

Exit Ticket

1. Example: Rectangle 8 units long and 3 units wide. Perimeter = 2 × (8 + 3) = 22 units; Area = 8 × 3 = 24 square units. The perimeter is twice the sum of length and width because both sides appear twice.

2. Possible dimensions: 3 × 8 → Perimeter = 22; 4 × 6 → Perimeter = 20. Both have an area of 24 but different perimeters.

Section 3: Representing Data with Line Plots
(4.MD.4; BEST MA.4.DP.1.1; TEKS 4.9A)

Fill in the Blanks

1. 2

2. $2^3/_4$

3. number line; top

Multiple Choice

1. b) To plot equivalent fractions accurately

2. c) 0

3. b) 1/8

Short Answer

1. To plot both on a line plot with quarter-inch intervals, convert 1/2 into fourths: 1/2 = 2/4. Now 1/2 and 1/4 can be placed correctly since both share the same denominator.

2. The most frequent value is 2/8 because it appears twice. Since there are 4 data points total, the fraction is 2/4, or 1/2.

3. The number line must be divided into eighths so fractions like 3/8 can be placed exactly. If you used fourths instead, 3/8 could not be plotted accurately.

Open Response

Line plot data: 1¼, 1½, ¾, 1, and 1¼. Two students are at 1¼, one at 1½, one at ¾, and one at 1. To compare, the total for two students: 1¼ = 1¼ + 1¼ = 2½. The one student at ¾ read ¾ hour. The difference is 2½ − ¾ = 1¾ hours more. The line plot helps visualize how the taller stack of X's at 1¼ represents greater total time than a single X at ¾.

Exit Ticket

1. Line plot: data points at ¼ (1 mark), ½ (2 marks), and ¾ (1 mark). Quarter intervals are used because all data values are multiples of ¼, keeping spacing equal and accurate.

2. Total: ¼ + ½ + ¾ + ½ = 2.

Section 4: Understanding Angles
(4.MD.5-7; BEST MA.4.GR.1.1; TEKS 4.7C)

Fill in the Blanks

1. right

2. center or center point

3. straight

Multiple Choice

1. d) Straight

2. b) Obtuse

3. a) 60°

Short Answer

1. An acute angle measures less than 90°, like a 45° angle. An obtuse angle measures more than 90° but less than 180°, like a 120° angle.

2. To sketch a 135° angle, start by drawing a 90° right angle using a protractor. Then measure and add another 45° beyond the 90° mark to reach 135°.

3. A straight angle measures 180°. It's additive because 45° + 135° = 180°, showing that the two smaller angles together form one straight line.

Open Response

The pizza is cut into four slices with angles of 30°, 90°, 120°, and 120°. The 30° slice is acute, the 90° slice is right, and the two 120° slices are obtuse. When you add them all together, 30 + 90 + 120 + 120, you get 360°, which makes a full circle, or one whole pizza.

Story example: "My friends and I shared a pizza that was cut into four uneven slices. I grabbed the 120° slice, which was the biggest! My friend took the 30° slice and couldn't believe how small it was. The 90° slice went to someone in the middle, and the last 120° slice went to the hungriest person. We realized that the bigger the angle, the larger the slice, because each degree represents a portion of the whole circle – and more degrees means more pizza!"

Exit Ticket

1. A 75° angle is acute because it's less than 90°. To measure it, place the center of the protractor on the vertex, align one ray with 0°, and read where the other ray crosses the scale at 75°.

2. 160° − 70° = 90°. One angle is 70° (acute) and the other is 90° (right).

Chapter 8: Classifying Shapes

Section 1: Identifying and Classifying Two-Dimensional Figures (4.G.1-2; BEST MA.4.GR.1.2; TEKS 4.6D)

Fill in the Blanks

1. trapezoid

2. obtuse

3. 360

Multiple Choice

1. c) Rectangle

2. c) Trapezoid

3. a) Acute; smaller than 90 degrees

Short Answer

1. In a parallelogram, both pairs of opposite sides are parallel, shown by arrow marks on each pair. In a trapezoid, only one pair of opposite sides is parallel, so the shape leans on one side instead of staying even on both.

2. A rectangle and a rhombus are both types of parallelograms because they each have two pairs of parallel sides. A rectangle has four right angles, while a rhombus has four equal sides.

3. A square has all right angles like a rectangle and all equal sides like a rhombus, so it fits the definition of both shapes.

Open Response

The shape could be a rectangle (or a square). It has two pairs of parallel sides and four right angles, which matches the definition of a rectangle. A square is also possible because it is a special type of rectangle with all sides equal.

Exit Ticket

1. A square has 4 parallel sides (2 pairs), 4 right angles, and a total interior angle sum of 360. It is also a rectangle because all its angles are right angles and opposite sides are parallel and equal.

2. A quadrilateral with four equal sides but no right angles is a rhombus. You can tell because all sides are congruent, and its opposite angles are equal, but the angles are not 90 degrees.

Section 2: Symmetry and Patterns (4.G.3; BEST MA.4.GR.1.3; TEKS 4.6B)

Fill in the Blanks

1. equal

2. 6

3. 2

Multiple Choice

1. d) Infinite

2. c) Rectangle (not a square)

3. a) It can be divided into two matching halves

Short Answer

1. A heart shape has only one line of symmetry because it can only be folded down the middle to make two equal halves; folding in any other direction does not match both sides.

2. An equilateral triangle has three lines of symmetry. Each line runs from a vertex to the midpoint of the opposite side, dividing the triangle into two equal mirror halves.

3. I disagree. A rectangle has two lines of symmetry—one horizontal and one vertical through the center. It does not have four because the diagonals do not create matching halves unless the rectangle is a square.

Open Response

For the school event logo, I designed a butterfly with two wings. I drew a vertical line down the middle to show one line of symmetry. When I fold along this line, both sides match exactly. Symmetry is important because it creates balance and makes designs look neat and organized.

Exit Ticket

1. Example: A heart or an isosceles triangle with a single vertical line down the middle marking one line of symmetry.

2. False. Only squares have four lines of symmetry. Rectangles that are not squares have two lines of symmetry (one horizontal and one vertical) because their sides are not all equal in length.

Index